The RAVEN & The TOTEM

By John Smelcer

Illustrated by Larry Vienneau and Susie Bevins

A SALMON RUN BOOK™

Anchorage

MADE IN U.S.A.

Cover design by Larry Vienneau
Artwork copyright 1992 by Larry Vienneau
and Susie Bevins

Library of Congress Cataloging-in-Publication Data:

Smelcer, John E. 1963-
        The Raven and the Totem.
        Bibliography:p.
        Includes Index.
        1. Alaska native legends. 2. Oral narratives.
3. Folklore. 4. Myths. 5. Am. Indian—Alaska.
I. Title.
E99.E7N76   1992   92-146504

Design and technical assistance by Larry Vienneau,
Mary Shampine, and Wes Skinner and the staff at ASETS.

A SALMON RUN BOOK
P.O. Box 231081
Anchorage, Alaska 99523-1081

Printed in the United States

A portion of the procedes from the sale of this book
shall be given to the Smelcer Scholarship Fund, which
provides a tuition scholarship for Alaskan students
attending the University of Alaska Anchorage.

Preface

This volume contains ethnographic narratives from the following Alaska native groups: Tlingit, Eskimo (Yupik, Sugpiaq, Inupiaq), and Athabaskan Indians. <u>Volume II</u>, to be published within the next couple years, will include "folktales" from the Aleut, Haida, Tsimshian, and Eyak linguistic groups.

Dedication

This book is dedicated to all Alaskan Natives whose magnificent oral narrative heritage is an inexhaustable source of inspiration and pride for the peoples of the world: the Haida, Tsimshian, Tlingit, Eyak, Alutiiq (Sugpiaq), Aleut, Siberian Yupik, Yupik, Inupiaq, Kutchin (Gwich'in), Han, Koyukon, Ingalik (Deg Hit'an), Holikachuk, Tanana, Upper Tanana, Tanacross, Tanaina (Dena'ina), Upper Kuskokwim, and Ahtna (of which my family belongs).

Acknowledgements

This book is the product of years of thought, research, collecting, drafting, revising and editing. During that time, many scholars and friends alike have influenced the ultimate production of this text. I would like to thank as many as I can for their particular role in this collection:

Dr. Jack Bernet, Professor Emeritus of English and himself an author of an anthology of Alaska native literature, who was to have been one of the editors; for his instruction, dedication, and scrutinous attention to authenticity in documentation. It was he who first inspired my desire to write a book of this nature.

Tom F. Sexton, M.F.A who agreed to be a reader of the manuscript even though he was overwhelmed by Creative Writing graduate students under his tutelage at University of Alaska Anchorage.

Larry Vienneau, M.F.A. for his wonderful artwork and cover design. This is our second book together in which his artistic talents have graced and enhanced my prose. He is both my good friend and a fellow outdoorsperson.

Susie Bevins, for her artwork. I was quite excited when I learned that she would consider illustrating several stories in this book. I am a great admirer of her work.

Dr. Robert Wilkinson for proofreading the Introduction, and Dr. O. W. "Jack" Frost for proofreading the manuscript for grammatical and syntactical errors.

Special gratitude to the University of Alaska Anchorage Consortium Library, particularly its Alaska Room, without whose kind assistance this collection would never have been. And thanks to Dick Howe of Best Electronics for the very fine laser printing job.

Lastly, I thank my friends: the Stuarts, Adams, Haymans-Edwards, and Dr. Jim Brown, for their moral support and recreational distractions during the project; and my family: Charles and Marie Smelcer, Herbert Smelcer, the entire Maslyk and Shampine family; and finally my wife, Pamela, and daughter Zara, for always encouraging my work, acting as sounding-boards for my ideas, and for loving me and giving me the support I needed for such an undertaking.

Contents

Athabaskan

For Zara Rhyana and Pamela Ann

Introduction

There are twenty Alaska native languages. Eskimo-Aleut is one language family, with Aleutian Aleut as one branch, and Eskimo at the other. There are four Eskimo languages in Alaska, three of them Yupik (Alutiiq [Sugpiaq], Central Yupik, and Siberian Yupik), and the other Inupiaq. Athabaskan-Eyak-Tlingit is another language family, with the nearly extinct Eyak as one branch and all the Athabaskan languages as another. Tlingit is in some ways distantly related to both. There are eleven Athabaskan languages in Alaska, differing to each other in varying degrees. Haida is a completely different language, spoken also in Canada. Tsimshian is also a completely different language, spoken mostly in Canada.

None of the Alaska native languages were written before the coming of the Russians.

Each Alaska native language has its own intricate beauty, a highly complex and regular grammar and enormous vocabulary. This has been developed by the people over the thousands of years they have lived in this area.

Recently the history of these languages has been tragic. From about 1900 until the 1960s, native languages were severely depressed. Children were punished for speaking their native language in school. They were forced to abandon their language, in order to speak English only. In 1972, the Alaska State Legislature passed the Bilingual Education bill, giving children the right to use and cultivate their native language in school, and also established the Alaska Native Language Center at the University of Alaska, Fairbanks. Many important developments are taking place now to maintain for future generations of Alaskans the precious heritage of their native languages and cultures.

—Taken from: Krauss, Michael E. Native Languages and Peoples of Alaska (Map). Fairbanks: Alaska Native Language Center, 1974. Revised 1982.

In the past several decades, the Alaska Native Language Center has indeed been the most significant preserver of both Alaska native languages and its cultural heritage. Besides the many scholarly studies, reports, conferences, and language texts, it has also either produced or participated in the publication of numerous collections and translations of native oral narratives, what is often loosely refered to as folklore, myths, and legends.

Many of the books I used as reference during my research and collection process, all of which are listed in the bibliography, were produced by the Alaska Native Language Center. Those most responsible for the success of the A.N.L.C. are Michael Krauss, Lawrence Kaplan, and James Kari. In almost every recently published text I discovered in the literature review, one of their names appeared somewhere in the acknowledgements. I owe a great debt to them as do the native peoples of Alaska for their careful and meticulous documentation and preservation of these oral texts and translations.

In the Fall semester of 1987, I was enrolled in Dr. Jack Bernet's Alaska Native Oral Narratives course at the University of Alaska Fairbanks. As one side of my family is Alaska Athabaskan, I instantly took an interest in the subject. For the next several years I thought about writing this collection. To that end, I made contact with several native corporations which were set up after ANSCA, and began my research.

Many of the "stories" assembled in this anthology are the result of comparative examination, that is the close examination and comparison of previously recorded tellings or narratives. The many stories presented here represent but a small portion of the total sum of all Alaskan ethnographic accounts published world-wide. In my research, I read and compared no less than 148 texts containing perhaps more than a thousand different stories and variations of Alaska native oral narratives. While much of my research came from these studies, a large number of tales were told to me by native Alaskans from rural communities. A few tales, I believe, have never been documented prior to this text and I am very excited to bring them into print where they can be preserved for future generations as Krauss suggests.

Whereas archaeologists can unearth artifacts to study past cultures, language does not preserve well in stratagraphic sequences due to its ethereal nature. Language, in non-written form, survives only by successful transmission to living generations.

Unfortunately, some Alaska native languages have very few surviving speakers. In 1982, only two or three native speakers of Eyak still lived. Anna Nelson Harry died in February of 1982 and in February of this year, Sophie Borodkin died in Cordova leaving only her sister, 73-year-old Marie Smith, as a remaining native speaker of the language. Besides her, only Michael Krauss still speaks Eyak. In 1982, only 20 speakers of Han and Holikachuk, both Athabaskan languages, survived, and less than a hundred speakers of Haida, Ingalik (Deg Hit'an), Tanaina (Dena'ina), and Tanacross existed. The urgency to preserve and cultivate these languages and their linguistic and cultural heritage is only too real; the immediacy only too conspicuous.

With this in mind, I set out some years ago to collect oral narratives so that they could be preserved, as authentically as possible, so that these wonderful tales, these stories, these myths and legends could be saved so that scholars and laymen alike could experience the magic and awesome power of these accounts which the natives of Alaska have passed on to successive generations for hundreds, perhaps even thousands of years.

As an Adjunct Professor of English at the University of Alaska Anchorage, I have met many adult native students from rural Alaska who were only too glad to share with me the stories their parents' parents had told them. In the summer of 1991, I was the Head Teacher of the Della Keats Summer Enrichment Program, held each year in Anchorage. It is a superb opportunity for young rural Alaska natives to experience several weeks actually studying and living in a college environment, while at the same time preparing themselves academically for careers in the Health Sciences. I too learned from the experience, making many friends who passed on to me the narratives they remembered from their parent's story-telling.

There are many good publications on the market and available in community libraries which fairly and accurately record native legends. There are some, however, which are of poor quality and exhibit sub-standard documentation techniques. Such data collection is abominable and does nothing to preserve cultural heritage. The "stories" in this collection have repeatedly undergone examination for authenticity. Several well-known Alaskan scholars and authors reviewed the original manuscript in an attempt to corroborate its authenticity.

It is important, at this point, to comment on the nature of the ownership of these narratives. Whereas it is hoped that people all over the world will read and enjoy these tales, the original ownership of these accounts belongs not to me or my publisher, but to the Alaska natives themselves. Indeed, in Tlingit society, their mythological and legendary tales are quite literally owned by specific clans. Therefore, should the reader delight in these narratives, then it is the native story-tellers to whom thanks should be directed. For any errors or mistakes in the text, I alone am responsible.

Some of the proceeds from the sale of this book are earmarked for a scholarship to encourage rural natives to attend college. Perhaps there they will learn of means to preserve and enhance their own heritage and take that knowledge back to their communities; in such a way their language and their "stories" will never perish from this earth.

— John E. Smelcer
Anchorage, 1992

3

Alaska Native Languages And Peoples

Alaska Quarterly Review, Teacher's Guide.
  Special Issue. Vol. 4 No. 3 & 4. Anchorage:
  Alaska Humanities Forum, 1988.

TLINGIT

The Creation Legend

Like many legends, in the beginning of time the world was only water; land had to be made before mankind could be created. As in other times, this duty fell to Raven.

A very long time ago, Raven was flying over the big waters and saw a beautiful fish woman swimming below. Raven fell in love with her and flew down to ask her to marry him. The fish woman was happy to see him, but before she would marry him she made him agree to one condition.

"I will marry you, Raven," she said, "if you will make some land so that I don't have to swim all of the time and I can dry my hair on the beach."

Raven agreed to her request and flew away to make land. He wanted someone to help him so he went to find help.

He flew around until he found a seal swimming in the warm waters.

"Seal," said Raven, "I need some sand from the bottom of the sea. Will you dive down and bring up some for me?"

Raven was very clever and did not tell the seal what he wanted the sand for.

Seal replied, "I will have to ask Frog for the sand."

Raven thought for a moment and said, "If you will ask Frog to get the sand for me, I will grant you both a favor."

"Oh," said Seal, "I'd like to have a shiny, warm coat of fur to keep me warm instead of these slimy scales. Then I could swim in the colder waters and keep warm."

Raven promised Seal the fur coat if he'd get the sand for him. At once Seal dived to the bottom of the sea where he found Frog. He told him of Raven's request and promise to grant them both a favor.

Frog told Seal, "Tell Raven that if he wants my sand he will have to make me Keeper-of-the-Earth's-Treasures, once and for all."

Seal was amazed at such a request but told it to Raven who was also amazed.

"That's asking for a lot," Raven said, "but tell Frog that if he gives me the sand I will grant his request."

With that, Seal again dived down deep to speak with Frog, all the while wishing that he had asked for more than just a fur coat.

When he told Frog that Raven agreed, Frog filled an old frogskin with sand and gave it to Seal.

As soon as Raven had the sand, he flew high into the air where the wind was blowing the strongest. Then, he opened the frogskin and cast the sand into the wind where it was scattered to all four corners of the world. Every place that a grain of sand landed, an island was formed. Some islands were bigger than others because the sand grain it was made from must have been bigger than others.

Once the land was made, the fish woman walked on the beach and dried her hair for the first time in her life. She agreed to marry Raven, and from their marriage came the great Raven clan.

For their help, Seal received a warm fur coat and Frog became the guardian of the earth's treasures.

Fire Legend

Having made the land with sand from the sea bottom, Raven made man next. Afterwards, he decided that man needed fire to cook with and to keep warm.

After making land, Raven decided to make man. He took clay and sand from the beach and formed the first man.

When he was done, Raven decided to fly around the entire world to see what he had created. While on this journey, Raven wondered if there was anything he should give man to make his life easier. Then he realized that he had forgotten to give man fire so that he could cook his food and keep warm.

Raven called to his friends, the other birds, and asked if they knew how to get fire. Seagull said that he had seen fire once at the Valley of Ten Thousand Smokes, what is now called Katmai, and so Raven asked for a volunteer to bring it to him.

Wood Owl agreed because he had a longer bill than the other birds and could safely carry a firebrand without burning his feathers.

The other birds and Raven agreed, even though they were jealous of the small owl's long bill.

So Wood Owl flew far across the waters to the Land of Ten Thousand Smokes, which is actually a large number of small volcanoes. The air was so hot that some of Wood Owl's feathers were singed.

He found a long firebrand and picked it up in his very long bill and began to fly back to where man lived. But, before he got there, the firebrand began to burn his bill. Wood Owl wanted to drop the burning stick into the sea.

Just then Raven flew close and shouted, "Don't drop the firebrand! If you do, it will surely go out in the water."

So the small owl kept flying even though his bill was being burned and it hurt very much. Finally, Wood Owl and Raven arrived at the place where man lived and dropped the burning stick so that man could cook and keep warm.

The fire had burned all of Wood Owl's bill so that only a small beak was left. The heat had singed his wings so that he could no longer take long journeys, and the smoke changed his voice so that he could make only a shrill whistle. This is how all of his descendants became as they are.

How Raven Brought Fire

This brief story is somewhat similar to the previous one, but a hawk, instead of the wood owl brings the fire and loses his long bill.

A very long time ago, Raven, while flying, saw something floating on the water. He looked at it and thought that it looked like fire and so he flew close to it and saw that it was a burning branch.

Raven called all of the birds and they gathered on the shore to listen to the great Raven speak.

"One of you must fly out there and bring that fire to me," said the black Raven.

He looked at the birds and chose the hawk to get the fire, because in those days hawks had long bills.

"Fly out there and bring the branch to me, and if it is hot do not let it go," he told Hawk.

So Hawk flew out to the firebrand on the water and grabbed it in his long bill. Then he started to fly back to where Raven and the other birds were gathered. By the time he got back, the hot fire had burned his bill down to nothing. Only a little beak was left. This is why hawks have a short beak today.

Fog Woman

This story depicts the creation of salmon and fog. Too,
it illustrates how men must treat wives with kindness
and respect. I have recorded similar accounts of this
legend in Tanaina and Tsimshian.

One day Raven decided to get married, so he flew to the
Tlingit chief, Fog-Over-The-Salmon, who had a beautiful young
daughter of marrying age.

The chief was happy that Raven wanted to marry his daughter
but he said, "You must first promise to take good care of my
daughter and to have respect for her. If you treat her badly, she
will leave you and never return."

Raven listened carefully to Fog-Over-The-Salmon and agreed to
his demands and they were soon married. Raven flew to his village
near the water with his bride on his back, and they lived there
all summer and fall. When winter came they were without food and
they grew very hungry.

One rainy day, after they had not eaten for some time, Raven's
wife began to make a large basket.

"What are you making a basket for?" asked Raven. "We have
nothing to put in it."

His wife did not answer him, but kept on making the basket
which was very large now.

That night they went to bed hungry again. But the next morning
when Raven woke up he saw his wife sitting on the floor with her
hands in the basket, which was full of water. He looked to see
what she was doing and when she was done there were salmon in the
basket! She had created the very first salmon!

Raven was very happy and so they cooked and ate the fish.
Thereafter, every morning she did the same thing, and every
morning the basket was full of salmon. Raven was never hungry and
their house was full of drying salmon.

Soon, though, Raven began to quarrel with his young wife and
forgot all the wonderful things she did for him. Every day he
fought with her more and more until he struck her with a large
piece of dried salmon. He had forgotten the words of Chief
Fog-Over-The-Salmon, and was treating her very badly.

Because of Raven's mistreatment, the beautiful young woman ran
away along the beach. Raven gave chase and when he caught up, he
tried to hold her, but his hands went right through her as if she
was mist. She ran away again and Raven followed. Every time he
tried to grab her, though, his hands passed right through her and

11

she could not be stopped.

She ran into the water and all of the salmon that she had made and dried followed her. As she walked further into the water, her body began to turn into mist until she disappeared and became the fog.

Raven flew to his father-in-law, Chief Fog-Over-The-Salmon, and begged to have his wife returned to him.

The chief listened to Raven and then told him, "You promised to take care of my daughter and to give her respect. You did not keep your word and so she is lost to you and you cannot have her back."

Raven Turns Into A Woman

This story is a continuation of the previous one. Here, saddened by the loss of his wife, the Fog Woman, Raven turns himself into a woman to marry again.

After Raven's wife turned into fog and after his visit with Chief Fog-Over-The-Salmon, Raven left the village crying, "My wife, my wife!"

Coming to some trees, he saw sap running down the bark and thought that it was sad and crying just as he was.

"Why, you are just like me," he said to the tree.

Still crying for his loss of the Fog Woman, Raven went to another place and turned himself into a woman. Then he thought to himself, "I must get married and have someone to look after me. But to get a good husband I must say that my father was a great chief. Whose daughter shall I say I am?"

Raven looked around until he saw a seagull sitting on a high rock. Long ago chiefs always sat at a high place in the morning to overlook the village. The seagull reminded Raven of a chief so he decided to call him self the daughter of the seagull.

"From now on," he said to himself, "I will call myself Sitter-on-the-High Cliff's daughter!"

Later, a canoe filled with men of the Killer Whale clan who were returning to their village passed Raven who was standing on the shore. Raven waved to them. because he was a beautiful woman the men stopped and talked. Soon, Raven had convinced one of the men to marry him.

The canoe continued its trip to the village with the Raven along this time. When it came close to the village, a man on he beach saw it and shouted, "Where is your canoe coming from?"

One of the men of the Killer Whale clan in the canoe answered, "We have been searching for a wife, and we have found her."

"Which chief's daughter is she?" asked the other people of the village when they arrived. They all knew that she must be the daughter of a chief because in those days men never went to get a woman by canoe unless she was the daughter of a chief.

"It is the daughter of Sitter-on-the-High Cliff," replied the men of the Killer Whale clan. All of the villagers believed this and so Raven's plan was working.

Raven made himself at home in the Killer Whale clan's house. Soon, though, the men noticed that their food was disappearing very quickly, even though they were good hunters and always had plenty of fish and grease.

They began to talk among themselves by the fire at night when Raven was asleep.

"What is wrong?" they asked. "What has become of our food and the boxes of grease and fat we had stored?"

They searched but they could not find out what was happening to them for a long time.

Raven wore a labret, an ornament worn in the lip, and it had beautiful abalone shells on it and was very valuable. One day, the men of the Killer Whale clan found the labret in one of the empty grease boxes and said, "Look at this labret. We know who owns it!" And so they went to ask the Raven how it got to be in the empty box.

When Raven saw the men with his labret he exclaimed, "Oh, my beautiful labret! That is the way with my labret, it just leaves my lip and goes off on its own whenever it wants to!"

Because he seemed so sincere, the Killer Whale people believed him.

Some time later, Raven said told the people of the Killer Whale clan, "I have been having very bad dreams. I dreamed that all of the people of the village were alseep, and that my husband went to sleep too and never awoke. My dreams always come true. Whatever I dream will certainly come true."

The people looked at each other and were very frightened by what Raven had told them.

Late that night, when everyone was asleep, Raven got a sharp stick and crept to where her husband slept, and killed him!

The next morning when the villagers woke up they heard Raven crying, "Oh, my husband! My husband!" Using his cunning, Raven told them that her husband's last words were to take his body away from the village and to provide for his wife while she mourned for him. The Killer Whale people did this.

Raven said, "When you hear me crying, I don't want any of you to pass the place where I am mourning. Leave me alone to cry in peace. You people must wait on me and bring me everything I eat. Also, you must paint my face black because I am a widow."

They had to do everything she told them. These are the rules that people have observed from that time.

Raven stayed there pretending to mourn for a long time and was fed by the Killer Whale clan and had a very easy life. And whenever anyone heard her crying near the place where her husband's body had been laid, no one dared to go near.

Raven lived there for a long time. But he did not cry because of his husband's death, but because of joy because he had tricked the people and had an easy life.

The Prince And The Salmon People

Like so many other didactic legends, this tale explains
why certain rituals and practices must be adhered to.

In the days of long ago, there was a prince named Yaloa who
lived with his parents in a village upriver from the sea. Yaloa
was a member of the killer whale clan, and it was tradition of
his people to be taught the ways of the sea by his mother's
brother. Yaloa was not very interested in this, but wanted to
learn the ways of the eagle and so he spent a great deal of time
trying to catch eagles.

Yaloa's mother wanted him to learn the ways of the killer
whale clan and urged him to practice the ways of the river and
the sea. Yaloa wanted to please his mother and so he learned to
catch salmon, but his heart was not in it. Instead, Yaloa tried
to catch eagles most of the time.

Once, he was lucky and caught a very large salmon. His mother
was proud of him and she carefully cut and dried it for him to
show his uncle when he came to teach him the ways of the sea.
Yaloa's mother told him that he must return the bones of the
salmon to the river where it was caught, as was the custom of
their people.

Yaloa did not want to do this and had his younger brother take
the bones to the river. His brother was not careful and only some
of the bones were returned to the river.

The next year the salmon run was very small and the people of
the village did not have enough salmon to feed themselves. That
winter starvation threatened Yaloa and his people. His younger
brother was very hungry and so Yaloa gave him a piece of dried
salmon that his mother was saving.

When his mother saw that part of the salmon was missing, she
thought that Yaloa had selfishly eaten it while the rest of the
village starved. Yaloa ran away in shame to the river. Some
people called to him from their canoe and took him to the land of
the salmon spirits. His mother, not knowing what happened,
thought that he must have drowned in the river.

Yaloa lived with the salmon people for a year and they taught
him the ways of the salmon and why it was important to return all
of the salmon's bones to the river. When this was not done, the
salmon people suffered and would not return to the river. Because
Yaloa had not returned all of the big salmon's bones to the
river, the chief of the salmon people was very sick. This was the
reason why the salmon run had been very poor.

15

Soon it was time for the salmon to return to the river and Yaloa went with them in the shape of a salmon. The people of Yaloa's village caught many fish and Yaloa was caught by his mother. She did not recognize him until she saw that he was wearing Yaloa's necklace. A shaman was asked to change Yaloa back to his human form, and in a few days he was human again.

Since Yaloa had learned so much about the salmon people, he went to find the missing bones so that the chief of the salmon people would be well again, and so that the salmon would return in large numbers. Yaloa taught his people all that he had learned from the salmon people. He taught them how to observe the rituals which pleased the salmon people.

In honor of his return and because of the knowledge he gave his villagers, a feast was given for Yaloa. Yaloa wanted to have many eagle feathers to give to his guests, so once again he went to hunt eagles. This time he used the skills taught to him by the salmon people. Yaloa turned himself into a salmon and when a eagle swooped down to get him with his sharp talons, Yaloa quickly turned back into a human and grabbed the eagle.

Although Yaloa caught many eagles this way, he was not happy because he longed to return to the salmon people. The day before the feast Yaloa changed himself into a salmon again and swam down the river to the salmon people's village and never went back to his mother's village.

The Giant Who Became Mosquitos

I have collected a number of very different versions of this particularly rare legend. The early 1900's version recorded in Juneau by Livingston F. Jones is perhaps the most accurate, and thus I rely considerably upon its merit.

A long time ago, longer than anyone can remember, there lived a giant savage who was very bloodthirsty and killed many young men so that he could drink their blood.

Many men tried to kill the giant but none ever could. All who went to battle the savage were killed. Once, three brothers decided to stop it and went to the mountains where it was said to live. The oldest brother took his weapons and went to seek the creature alone. After a day he did not return and so the next brother went to kill the savage giant. He was killed, too.

Then, the youngest brother took his bow and arrow and traveled to the place where his brothers had gone.

The place was high in the mountains and there were large boulders all about. The young warrior moved from rock to rock, hiding behind each boulder as he hunted the giant.

Suddenly a shadow was cast over him and as he looked up he saw the giant man's terrible club crashing down upon his head. When he awoke, he was inside a large game bag and was being carried towards a cave in the mountainside where the savage lived.

The young man felt around in the dark and found his cutting stone and with it he sliced through the bag so that he could escape. His bow and arrows fell out, too. Instantly the young warrior grabbed them and hid behind a rock.

The giant kept walking to his cave thinking that he still had his dinner in the bag. The young man followed him, even though it was hard to keep up because the giant took such long steps.

When they arrived at the cave he saw the bodies of his brothers and of many other men from his village. The giant had killed them all and drank their blood!

The giant dropped the game bag in a corner of the cavern and leaned his large and heavy club, which was as thick as a tree, against the cave wall.

When the savage turned around the young man pulled back hard on his bow and let his best arrow fly through the air at the giant's heart.

The sharp arrow hit him in the chest and he started to bleed. But before dying the giant said, "Though you killed me, I will

18

still drink your blood."

The young man gathered wood and brush and dragged the giant's dead body to the pile and placed it on top. Then he rubbed his fire-making sticks together until the sparks made the dry kindling catch fire. Soon the whole pile was burning brightly. It burned for a long time until only ashes remained of the blood-thirsty savage.

Then the young man took the ashes and threw them high into the air. The wind blew the ashes all over the world and each piece of ash turned into a mosquito. That is why mosquitoes are hungry for blood—because they were made from the ashes of the bloodthirsty giant.

Beaver And Porcupine

As with numerous myths and legends, this story depicts an event which led to the present state of a natural condition. A similar account is told in Tsimshian.

In the days of long ago, before the Tlingit lived, Porcupine and Beaver were very good friends and visited one another. Although Porcupine visited Beaver's house often, Beaver did not like how Porcupine always left many sharp quills when he left. So one day Beaver decided that he wasn't going to invite Porcupine to his home anymore.

One day Porcupine told Beaver that he wanted to come and visit.

"I will take you on my back to my house on the lake," said Beaver.

But when Porcupine climbed on to his back, Beaver did not take him directly to his house like he always did. Instead, he took him to a large tree stump in the middle of the lake and told Porcupine to climb off his back.

"This is my house," said Beaver as he swam away, leaving Porcupine stranded on the stump.

At first Porcupine didn't know why his friend had done this to him or how he was going to get off the stump. So he used his powers to get off.

"Make the lake become frozen," he sang over and over again.

After a short time the lake became frozen! Porcupine climbed off the stump and onto the frozen lake and walked safely to shore.

Later, Porcupine met Beaver in the woods and said, "I would like you to visit my house now. I will carry you on back."

So Beaver got onto his friend's back and Porcupine climbed to the very top of a very high tree.

Then Porcupine told Beaver that this was his house and so Beaver climbed off his back.

When he was off, Porcupine climbed down and left Beaver stranded at the top of the tree just like he he was left stranded on the tree stump on the lake. For a long time Beaver could not get down and was stuck there. Finally, though, he was able to slide down the tree using his sharp teeth and claws to keep him from falling. This is how lines got in the tree bark.

Frog Woman

The story of the Frog Woman is an old one which depicts the birth of the Frog Clan. I have come across several versions of this legend. The following two accounts represent the two most common of these.

There was a big village in the Yakutat country. Beside the village was a big lake with many frogs. In the middle of the lake there was a grassy place where the frogs gathered.

One day, the young daughter of the village chief was walking along the lake. She was making fun of the frogs and picked up one large frog in her hand and spoke to it.

"There are so many of you. You must live as we live in our village," she said.

"You must eat and sleep together as we do in our houses," she continued.

That very night, when the young girl went for a walk, a handsome young man came to her.

"Will you marry me?" he asked her.

The chief's daughter had turned away other young men before, but she wanted to marry this one. He turned towards the lake and pointed.

"There's my father's house, where we will live and eat and sleep together."

Together they walked to the lake. When they came to the very edge, it lifted up like a door and they could see the entire muddy bottom of the lake. They walked under it.

The chief's daughter became one of the frog people and was not heard of until the next spring when a man from the village saw her in the middle of the lake. There she sat right in the middle with a bunch of frogs. The man ran back to the village and told the chief what he had seen.

The village people and the chief went to the lake and asked the frog people to give back the young girl, but the frogs refused. Then the father thought up a plan. The village men dug deep trenches to empty the water out of the lake.

As the water left the lake, frogs were scattered everywhere. The chief's daughter came floating down and some people grabbed her and she was taken back to the village. They hung her upside down to get all of the mud out of her which she had eaten while living with the frog people. After this she could not eat anything, and she could not speak their language any more. Instead, she made sounds like a frog.

The girl died soon after returning to the village. But because of what happened, the people there have always felt close to the frog people and they understand their ways. The frogs there can even understand what the people of the village say to them. The Tlingit of the Yakutat area have songs from the frogs, and frog names and emblems.

The Girl Who Was Taken By The Frog People

This particular telling of the Tlingit legend of "The
Frog Woman" is very similar to J. R. Swanton's account
which he collected in 1904 outside Wrangell. Although
there are some differences, it is quite similar.

There was a large town in the Yakutat country and not too far
away there was a big lake full of frogs. In the middle of this
lake there was a large swampy place where many frogs used to sit.
One day the chief's daughter spoke badly to the frogs. She picked
up a large one and made fun of it, saying, "There are so many of
you living here. I wonder if you do things like we do. I wonder
if you get married and live together."
When she went out of her house that night, a young man came to
her and asked, "Will you marry me?" The chief's daughter had
rejected many men before, but she agreed to marry this one right
away.
Pointing towards the lake in the distance, the man said, "That
is where my father's house is and where we shall live together."
They walked to the lake and when they arrived, it seemed as
though the edge of the lake was lifted up like a blanket so that
they could go under it. They walked under it. So many young
people were there that she did not think about going home again.
Meanwhile, her father and friends missed her and looked for
her. But they did not think to look under the lake. Finally, they
gave up and beat the drums and had a death feast. They painted
their faces black and cut their hair as was their way.
In the spring, there was a village man who was going hunting
and so he went to the lake to bathe himself in urine so that he
could hunt better. When he was done he threw the urine into the
lake and it landed among some frogs sitting there and they jumped
into the water. The next day he did the same thing but this time
he saw the chief's daughter sitting in the swampy place in the
middle of the lake. He dressed quickly and ran to the village to
tell the chief what he had seen.
He told the girl's father and soon many villagers went to the
lake to see if it was truly the missing young woman. When they
saw that it was indeed her, the people brought gifts to trade for
the girl's release. But the frog people would not give her up. By
and by, the chief thought of a plan and he called all of the men
of the village together. Then he told them to dig trenches so
that they could empty the water of the lake. The frog chief could
see what they were doing and told his people.

23

The men worked and worked, dug and dug, until soon the lake water was almost gone. The frog chief asked the girl to tell the villagers to have pity on them and not to kill all of them. But the villagers only wanted the girl and didn't harm the others.

Soon, the frogs were scattered all over and the people caught the girl and her frog husband. They let the frog go and took the girl back to the village.

When anyone spoke to the girl, she made only popping sounds like a frog. But after a while she was able to speak again and she told them how all of the frog people of the lake had floated away in the trenches and were lost. The woman would not eat at all, even though they tried everything. After a while they hung her upside down and the black mud which she had eaten while among the frogs came out of her. When the last of the mud came out, she died.

Because this woman was taken away by the frogs of that place, and because she died there, the frogs of Yakutat can understand Tlingit and some of the people can understand them. Nowadays, the people have frog songs and frog names and the frog emblem.

Raven And Whale

Besides being a powerful, and sometimes troublesome bird, Raven is always hungry and since he is lazy, he often gets into trouble when he tries to get something for nothing.

As always, Raven was bored and wanted something to do. He didn't care if it was mischievous or not, he just wanted something to do.

One day while flying high in the air, he saw a whale swimming on the water letting the sunshine warm his back. Raven noticed herring eggs all over the whale's back, and since he was always hungry, he could not resist the eggs. He did not want them to be wasted, so he alighted on the whale's back and began eating the herring eggs. Soon, though, they were all gone and Raven was still hungry.

The warm sunshine made Raven tired and soon he fell asleep. When he awoke from his nap he was still hungry and so he asked the whale, "Do you have any other food for me to eat? I am still hungry even though I have eaten all the herring eggs."

The whale answered that he had no more food. But Raven kept asking if he had more food.

"No," said the whale. "I have nothing at all. Just leave me alone."

Raven kept asking and finally he asked if the whale had any food inside his mouth.

"What is inside your mouth? It is so big," he asked the perturbed whale.

The whale did not answer but grew tired and began to yawn. As soon as he did, Raven ran into his mouth to look for food. But soon he realized that there was nothing to eat and he wanted out, but the whale didn't open his mouth to let Raven out.

After several days of being stuck inside the whale, Raven grew to be very hungry. He cooked the whale's liver and ate it. But he was still hungry. Next, he took the whale's heart, cooked it, and ate it. The whale died because Raven had eaten his heart.

The next day the dead whale washed up on the beach. Raven was still inside and could not get out. He was getting very hungry again.

Some children from a nearby village were playing on the beach and saw the dead whale, but they did not go near it.

Several days later the same children were playing again and Raven started to yell so that they would hear and come nearer. He

25

pleaded with them to get him out of the whale.

The children were afraid but when they heard Raven's voice they listened. Raven told them that he was inside of the whale and that he wanted them to cut it open to let him out. The whale was so big that it took all the children to finally cut it open.

Finally, Raven stepped out and flew away, thanking them for helping him.

The Creation Of The Killer Whale

The Killer Whale clan is one of the most powerful of all Tlingit clans. This legend tells how Natsalane', a mighty Tlingit hunter, created the giant killer whale for revenge. As with most documented folklore, there are numerous variations which vary at different locals.

There was once a very strong and mighty Tlingit hunter, named Natsalane', who could throw a spear and shoot an arrow better than any other. When he hunted, he always killed the animal that he tracked. Whenever he returned from a hunt, the whole village would come see him because he always brought meat which he would share.

Now Natsalane' often hunted with his three brothers, and together they often prepared for hunts. One day the brothers were preparing for a seal hunt and they began to wonder.

"If it were not for Natsalane', we would be the mightiest hunters in the village and all of the people would come out to see us when we returned from a hunt," said the oldest of the brothers.

The other brothers agreed and they planned to kill Natsalane' while on the seal hunt.

The day the great hunt came, the hunters went to a small island which was exposed because the tide was low. But when the tide came in, the small island would be under water. Here they left Natsalane' to drown. As they paddled away, the youngest brother begged the others not to kill their brother by leaving him to drown.

"Please, do not do this terrible thing," he pleaded as he tried to turn the canoe around.

The young brother failed and they left the great hunter to drown on the island alone. Natsalane' watched as they faded in the distance and covered his face as the water rose.

Suddenly he heard a voice speaking to him. He opened his eyes but saw no one, only a loon floating nearby. Again he closed his eyes and again he heard the voice. This time he looked through his fingers and saw that it was the loon. Because loons are very hard to catch, Natsalane' was rewarded. The loon used his magic and made a hole in the water's surface. Under it was a place with people who spoke his language.

The chief of these people told Natsalane' that he could get to shore if he thought about reaching the beach and not about the island.

27

The hunter thanked him and began to swim to shore. But halfway he turned and thought about what had happened to the small island and he started to drown.

Quickly Natsalane' thought only about the beach and he soon made it there!

It took him a few days to reach his village. He snuck into his house at night and told his wife to get his tools for him. He also told her not to tell anyone that he was alive and well—especially not his brothers.

That very night Natsalane' took the tools and walked up the beach, far from the village, and began his plan for revenge. He fell a great tree and carved from it the most horrible, powerful monster he could and named it "Keet".

When he was finished, he sang and danced and spoke to it and pushed it into the sea. It was alive but it did not swim. In a few minutes it washed up on shore and died. But Natsalane' did not give up his plan. Instead, he fell a giant cedar and carved the horrible whale-monster again.

When he was done, he sang and danced and again named it "Keet". He pushed it into the water and it began to swim wildly showing its large, sharp teeth.

Natsalane' spoke, "I created you to kill my brothers who tried to kill me. Kill the two, but spare the youngest who tried to save me."

For some days Natsalane' and the killer whale waited and watched for the canoe of his brothers. Finally, the right canoe came by and the hunter told Keet to go do as he demanded.

Keet swam to the canoe as fast as an arrow, snapping his jaws and showing his terrible teeth. He killed the two brothers and smashed the canoe. Then he brought the youngest brother to shore.

Now that he had his revenge, Natsalane' thought that he must do something about Keet. He had created a monster which might kill many Tlingit.

Natsalane' spoke to the great killer whale, "I created you only to kill the people who had done a great wrong to me. Now I will let you go. Because I am a man, you are never to kill another man again. Go now and do not kill."

Keet looked at Natsalane' and he no longer looked terrible. It turned and swam slowly away as its maker watched.

The killer whale has never killed a man since then.

Raven Steals The Sun, Stars, And Moon

Just as western religion suggests that the world was void of light in the beginning, so too does this Tlingit tale in which Raven steals the sun, moon, and the stars and then releases them. There are similar documented ethnographic accounts in Eskimo, Upper Tanana, Tanaina, Koyukuk, Deg Hit'an, Ahtna, and Tsimshian mythology. In some versions Raven turns himself into a hemlock needle to impregnate a young woman, while in others he becomes a spruce needle, a small fish, and even a piece of fine moss.

In the beginning there was no moon or stars at night. Raven was the most powerful being. He had made all of the animals, fish, trees, and men. He had made all living creatures. But they were all living in darkness because he had not made the sun either.

One day, Raven learned that there was a chief living on the banks of the Nass River who had a very wonderful daughter who possessed the sun, the moon, and the stars in a carved cedar box. The chief and his people guarded her and the treasure well.

Raven knew that he must trick the villagers to steal their treasure, so he decided to turn himself into a grandchild of the great chief. Raven flew upon a tall tree over their house and turned himself into a hemlock needle. Then, as the needle, he fell into the daughter's drinking cup and when she filled it with water, she drank the needle. Inside the chief's daughter, Raven became a baby and soon the young woman bore a son who was dearly loved by the chief and was given whatever he asked for.

The stars, moon and the sun were each in a beautifully carved cedar box which sat on the wood floor of the house. The grandchild, who was actually Raven, wanted to play with them and wouldn't stop crying until the grandfather gave them to him. As soon as he had them Raven threw them up through the smokehole. Instantly, they scattered across the sky. Although the grandfather was unhappy, he loved his grandson too much to punish him for what he had done.

Now that he had tossed the stars and moon out the smokehole, the little grandson began crying for the box containing sunlight. He cried and cried and would not stop. He was actually making himself sick because he was crying so much. Finally, the grandfather gave him the box.

Raven played with the box for a long time. Suddenly, he turned himself back into a bird and flew up through the smokehole with the box.

Once he was far away from the village on the Nass River he heard people speaking in the darkness and approached them.

"Who are you and would you like to have light?" he asked them. They said that he was a liar and that no one could give light.

To show them that he was telling the truth, Raven opened the ornately carved box and let sunlight into the world. The people were so frightened by it that they fled to every corner of the world. This is why there are Raven's people everywhere.

Now there are stars, the moon, and daylight and it is no longer dark all of the time.

Raven Tricks Seagull And Crane

One of the chief roles played by Raven in many legends is his role as trickster, his ability to trick others through deceit. This story involves a fight orchestrated by Raven between Seagull and Crane. In earlier versions of this myth, there is a heron instead of a crane.

Raven was walking along a beach one day and as usual he was hungry. The water was full with herring but Raven wasn't a good fisherman, and besides, he was lazy and didn't want to work for his food. He had to think of a way to get the fish.

He looked around and saw a crane standing in the shallow water, fishing, and then he saw a sea gull sitting on a rock swallowing a fat herring he had just caught. Raven watched and could see the bulge in his chest that was made by the swallowed herring.

Raven thought to himself, "I must have that fish or I will starve."

He walked up to Crane and spoke to him, and then walked over to the seagull and spoke to him.

Returning to Crane he said, "I didn't want to tell you this, because it is none of my business, but I feel that I must because I am your friend. You saw me speaking to Seagull just now? He said that you are stupid and ugly and that all of your ancestors were slaves."

Crane looked over at Seagull but said nothing.

Then Raven walked over to Seagull again and spoke to him.

"You saw me talking to Crane just now? Well, I shouldn't tell you this, but he called you some very bad names and said even worse words about your ancestors," said Raven.

Seagull said nothing but looked over at Crane who was still standing in the water.

Then Raven walked back to Crane and spoke to him again.

"I think I should warn you, " he said, "that Seagull just told me that he was coming over here to fight with you. If he does, you must kick him hard in the chest. This is the only way to beat him."

Crane looked over at Seagull, who seemed restless and thanked Raven for the advice.

Then Raven went back to speak with Seagull and told him how Crane was very mad at him and wanted to fight him. Raven told Seagull how he should use his chest if Crane tries to kick him.

"Use your chest because it is strong and he cannot hurt you there," said Raven.

Just then Crane shifted his feet because the one was getting tired.

"See!" said Raven, "He is preparing to come over here to fight you. You should attack first and don't forget to use your chest as a shield."

So Seagull and Crane began to fight with one another. Both were very grateful that their new friend, Raven, had warned them.

Crane kicked at Seagull and Seagull used his chest as a shield as Raven had said. When Crane's foot struck him, the hard jolt made the herring come out of Seagull's stomach. Raven caught it before it hit the water and flew away laughing at the two birds. Crane and Seagull realized that they had been tricked by Raven and stopped fighting.

Raven flew away looking for his next meal because he was still hungry.

How Cormorant Lost His Tongue

The mischievous Raven is always hungry and is always getting into trouble. In this tale of trickery and deceit, Raven shows his true colors.

It happened one day as Raven was flying away after tricking the sea gull out of herring, that he saw a small village and so he landed. As always, Raven was hungry again.

He still had some of Sea Gull's herring in his beak and he rubbed them on himself so that the shiny scales would stick to him. Then he walked into the village and pretended that he was very full from eating fish.

Raven rubbed his stomach and said to the villagers, "Oh, I am so full from eating. But there are still a lot of herring where I caught these."

The mischievous black bird pointed far away, telling the villagers that the fish were there. Because it was time for the herring run, the people believed him and rushed away to catch fish.

Now that the village was empty, Raven took his time and stole a large canoe and took whatever he wanted from the villagers who were all gone fishing.

After he had the canoe heavily loaded, he took Cormorant and Loon as slaves to paddle his craft for him. Cormorant was known as the black diver duck who could speak and sits on the rocks, and Loon was known as the bird who never flies except in the springtime. The Tlingit always knew when the herring run was in because Loon always called with his one lone cry when it was time.

The two slaves paddled the canoe while Raven ate the food he had taken when he tricked the villagers.

They came to another small village where there was a great number of halibut. Raven asked the people if he could have enough halibut for himself and his two slaves, but they told him to catch his own. They told him that there were many halibut right in front of the village and that all he had to do was fish for them himself.

Raven became ashamed of his laziness and with Cormorant he went fishing for halibut. But when they got to the place, Raven just sat and watch Cormorant fish. In no time Cormorant had filled the canoe with halibut and they started back to the village.

Now Raven had bragged to the people how great a fisherman he was, and he knew that he'd be disgraced if they learned that Cormorant caught all the fish while he just watched. Raven thought how he could stop them from knowing and then he had a plan.

"What is that on your tongue?" he asked Cormorant. "Stick it out and I will take a closer look."

Cormorant stuck out his tongue and instantly Raven grabbed it and pulled it out!

Then Raven said, "Let me hear you speak."

But Cormorant could not even though he tried.

When they arrived in the small village with their halibut, the people were amazed. As Raven picked up each of the large fish from the canoe, he told the villagers how he caught them. Cormorant jumped about and did his best to tell the people that it was he, not Raven, who caught the fish. But however hard he tried, he could not get them to understand what he was saying.

Raven kept pulling out halibut and telling the people how he had caught them. When he came to the last fish, a very big halibut, Raven told them how hard it was to land it and how he fought it for a long time.

Cormorant started jumping about even more, pointing and trying to tell them how he had caught the halibut.

Raven stopped talking and said, "See my slave? He is trying to tell you that I had a very hard fight with this one. I almost lost my life trying to get it into the canoe."

All of the people thought that Raven must surely be the greatest fisherman. The children even thought he was a great fisherman. But the cormorant to this day sits on rocks near the sea and cannot speak and has not had a tongue since Raven pulled it out long ago.

The Owl Legend

As are many native legends, this story is didactic. That is, it teaches a moral or lesson. The message here: Don't mistreat your mother-in-law and don't be selfish.

A young woman once lived with her husband and mother-in-law in a village where Sitka is today. The village was close to the sea and she often walked along the beach watching the waves crash upon the rocks. During the herring season, when the shallow waters were full of herring, she would watch how countless herring would be swept to shore by the tide but then would be washed away again as the tide receded.

She looked on and thought, "There must be some way to catch these fish so that I will have plenty of food. What a waste that they are washed away by the water."

She walked along the beach still thinking about the question. Just then she saw a dense patch of hemlock trees in the woods whose branches were so intertwined that they looked like a net.

This gave her an idea. She tore some branches from the hemlock tree and ripped some long strips of bark from a nearby cedar. Using the wet bark like string, she fastened the hemlock branches into a large basket-shaped net. With the basket in hand she walked to where the herring were and waited for the tide.

Finally, the tide came in and the fish were everywhere. She walked out in the sea up to her waist and dipped her basket into the waves.

"Come to your wife, fish," she said smiling.

When she brought it up, it was full of shiny herring. She carried the heavy basket onto the beach and poured the wiggling, shimmering fish onto the sand.

Then, with her basket-net empty, she returned to the same place and caught more fish. Every time she dipped the basket under the waves it came up full of fish. She was very happy because her idea worked so well.

When she had enough fish, she hid her invention in the woods where no one else would find it because she was greedy and did not want to share; especially with her mother-in-law. She decided that she wasn't even going to give her any of the fish to eat.

That night the young woman waited until the mother-in-law was out of the house, and then she cooked some of the herring for herself and ate them all. But the mother-in-law smelled the fish and came into the house.

"What are you cooking?" she asked. "It smelled so good outside. What are you eating?"

The young woman swallowed her last bite and answered. "Nothing," she said.

The next day when her husband was seal hunting she cokked another herring.

This time her mother-in-law came into the house before she had eaten all of he fish.

"I smell cooked fish again. You must be eating something. May I have something to eat?" asked the older woman.

Even though she had her basket-net and could catch many herring, the young woman was greedy and placed fish entrails onto the cooking stick and cooked them for the mother-in-law and gave them to her.

"My son shall hear of how you have mistreated me and would have me go without food!" shreiked the old lady.

The young woman only ignored her. She was going to have all the fish she wanted and she wasn't going to share with anyone. After all, she thought, it was she who had invented the fishing basket.

When her husband returned from seal hunting, the mother-in-law took him aside and told him about his wife's cruelty.

The husband did not speak to her and so she went fishing again, but she could not find her basket. She had forgot where she had hid it.

As darkness came she stood on the beach screaming, "Where is my basket? Give me my basket! Bring my basket!"

She could see that the water was full of herring but she could not catch any of them.

She stood there still screaming and her voice was growing hoarse. "Where is my basket? Bring me my basket!"

No one answered her and she could not find the basket and the fish were laughing at her.

The young woman kept screaming until she could no longer make words. Her voice changed until she could only say, "Whoo... Who...Whoo..." Her arms changed into wings as she became an owl!

She flapped her wings and flew away hooting, "Whoo...Whoo... Whoo..."

Today, when a young girl is greedy, her parents warn her that if she is selfish and mistreats her mother-in-law, that she will become an owl.

Shunyuxklax And The Salmon People

Salmon is the primary subsistence food of many native Alaskan groups. Because of this, they must never be insulted. This legend illustrates what happened when a young boy once insulted the people of the salmon tribe. In another version of this myth, the young boy's name is Auktatsi.

A long time ago, when Raven was still creating the world, there was a large village named Dahxeit where Sitka is today. There was a salmon stream that ran through the village and all the young boys played in it. One of their favorite games was to snare the sea gulls which stayed near the stream.

Once, after a poor day of sea gull snaring, the chief's son was hungry and so he yelled to his mother, "I'm hungry. Give me something to eat."

The mother gave him the dried bony shoulder piece of smoked salmon. The boy threw it on the ground and asked his mother, "Why do you always give me the part of the salmon which no one else will eat?"

Just then several other boys called to him saying that there was a sea gull in his snare. The chief's son ran to his snare, forgetting his hunger for the moment. He rushed into the water and grabbed the snare line which the sea gull was pulling further into the deep water of the salmon stream. The boy kept hanging on to the line until he was pulled into water over his head and he disappeared beneath the surface.

Under the water, on both sides of him, was an army of salmon men, all facing one direction. Their eyes stared at him. When they began marching, he went along with them.

Time passed, but none of the people ate any food even though their mouths were constantly moving.

The young boy was hungry and when he looked down he saw what looked like salmon eggs on the stream bottom.

"I wonder why they are not eating the salmon eggs," he thought. "I eat them at home. Why do they not eat them here as well? I will eat some when they are not watching."

He picked up a handful and ate them. Just then the salmon people yelled, "Shunyuxklax has eaten our dung! Shunyuxklax has eaten our dung!"

The chief's son couldn't believe it. He was hungry and instead of eating the dried bony shoulder his mother had given him, he had eaten salmon dung. Thus he learned to have respect for food and not to insult it as he had done. The salmon people gave him his Tlingit name, Shunyuxklax, because it is the name for that piece of salmon.

Shunyuxklax lived with the salmon people for years and had forgotten about his human form and his village. After four years, he became aware of a great movement in the salmon tribe, which had been living in the sea for many years. They each began to move towards the rivers and streams, searching for the place of their birth. Thousands of them started on the long and difficult journey. The ones in front jumped out of the water. When Shunyuxklax asked what they were doing, he was told that they were scouts who looked to see where they were.

On the way they met even more fish, some which were silvery, which were headed up the rivers. They were all excited and in a hurry and swam quickly. Shunyuxklax had never seen anything so crazy as they were.

Along the great journey, entire groups of the marching army would break off and swim away saying, "This is the way to our birth place."

Shunyuxklax kept swimming until he came upon the very stream where his family and relatives lived. The water was shallow and he could see many women along the shores cutting salmon to dry. There were men and boys standing in the water with spears. He could even see the house he had lived in before he joined the salmon people.

One of his fish friends said to him, "Your mother is over there. Why don't you go close to her?"

When he got close, he saw that it was his mother. Then he would rush back into the deeper water. Then he wanted to see her again so he went close to her again.

His mother called to her husband, "There is a fine young salmon that keeps coming close to me. Spear him so that we can eat him for dinner tonight."

Shunyuxklax heard this and it scared him, so he tried to get to the deeper water. But the husband, his father, speared him and handed him to his mother. The mother was about to cut off his head when she saw that the salmon wore a copper necklace just like the one their son wore before he was lost. Her husband took the fish and rolled it in a mat and placed it on a board near the roof of their house.

That night as the villagers sat around a fire, they heard someone singing. They looked around but saw nobody. A while later they heard it again. This time they looked around and saw that the mat was moving around. The father took the mat down and unrolled it. Instead of the salmon, they found the young boy who had been missing for so long. Shunyuxklax told the villagers about his experience with the salmon people.

His father gave him the same name and he was known far and wide because he was the boy who had been taken by the salmon tribe for insulting them. Tlingits do not insult the salmon because they come every year and bring food to the villagers.

Wolf And Wolverine

This particular legend, told by an elder in Seward, is reminiscent of the Western story of the race between the tortoise and the hare. Like that tale, it also instructs people not to be too proud or boastful.

The wolf was the fastest animal in the forest and he was always boasting how no other animal could run faster than he. He was always bragging how much faster he was than Wolverine because Wolverine's legs were so short.

One day Wolverine became tired of the insults and challenged Wolf to a race.

"We will run up to the top of the mountain and then back down," said Wolverine. "Whoever reaches the bottom first wins."

Wolf just laughed, knowing that he could easily out run the short-legged wolverine.

But Wolverine had a plan and knew that he would win, so he made a bet with Wolf.

"If I win, then you must bring me food to eat for the rest of the summer," he said to the bragging Wolf.

Wolf accepted the bet because he knew he would never lose to the wolverine.

"You are too slow to beat me," replied Wolf. "But I will race you just to show you who is faster."

As the two lined up to start the race, the other animals of the forest stood by and watched. Not one of them thought that Wolverine could win, but they cheered him on anyhow because they were all tired of hearing the wolf brag about how fast he was.

When the race began, both animals ran up the mountain. With his longer legs, the wolf ran with ease while the wolverine had to work hard because of his short legs.

Wolf reached the top and turned around to look down. Wolverine was a long ways away and the wolf laughed at him.

"You are too slow, Short Legs. You might as well give up now," he said taunting the poor, tired wolverine.

Just as Wolverine reached the top, Wolf Laughed at him once more and started down the mountain thinking how Wolverine would have to bring him food for the rest of the summer.

But when Short Legs reached the top, he quickly rolled himself into a furry ball and started rolling down the mountain. Just as a round rock rolls quickly down a hill, so too did Wolverine now.

He rolled faster and faster until he passed the surprised Wolf and won the race!

The wolf was very tired. All of the animals laughed at him because Wolverine had beat him. For the rest of the summer they all laughed at Wolf who had to bring food to the wolverine because he had beaten him in the race.

Beaver, Ground-Hog, And Brown Bear

This interesting story involves three unlikely characters who all take part in the creation of Klawock Lake. The legend also instructs people to listen to warnings and that we can learn from those smaller and weaker than ourself.

A long time before man ever lived, the animals lived in the world and had it all to themselves. But, like man, they were always fighting each other. The beaver and the brown bear were especially unfriendly to each other. The brown bear, because of his size and great strength, was always destroying the work of the beaver. The beaver was usually mad because he always looked forward to winter and put aside wood so that he would have plenty of food to eat when it became cold.

One day Brown Bear came upon a beaver dam which had only just been finished after months of hard work. The great bear decided to tear it down.

Beaver saw Brown Bear about to destroy the dam and he begged him not to. He told the bear how the dam was holding back a whole river of water which would flood the entire valley if it were broken. The valley was the home to many animals, including the bear himself whose cave was there. Ground Hog lived there, too, and his meadow would be destroyed if the dam was torn apart.

But Brown Bear didn't care about the beaver's words and he began to pull the logs from the dam with his long, sharp claws. Logs and branches flew everywhere while Beaver kept warning the mischievous bear to stop.

Suddenly, the walls of the dam gave in to the pressure of the water and it broke wide open. The surprised bear was carried down the valley by the rushing river of water and logs. When Beaver saw this he got his family safely to higher ground. But the other animals were not so fortunate. All the ground-hogs drowned except one, and all of the bears drowned in their caves, except the mischievous one who created the deadly avalanche of water in the first place.

As the rushing torrent finally slowed, the valley was filled with water and became a large lake. In the middle of the newly made lake was a very tired brown bear and a sopping wet ground-hog. The small ground-hog swam close to the bear and asked him where he was going.

"See those two mountain tops over there?" asked Brown Bear pointing straight ahead. "That is where I am going."

Ground-hog looked to the peaks and then turned to the bear.

"I cannot swim that far. I am half-drowned now. I will surely die if I try to swim that far," replied the panting ground-hog.

Brown Bear told him to grab on to his fur on the back of his neck and he would take him to the mountain top safely. Ground-hog agreed. It was better, he thought, to be eaten by a treacherous bear later than to drown now.

The bear swam easily with his large and powerful paws and the two were soon on dry land. But the bear had never before been in water above his knees and he didn't know how to get his fur dry other than to take his coat off and hang it in the sun to dry. This is the way bears had always dried their fur coats before the flood.

The ground-hog, on the other hand, knew a way to shed the water from his fur quickly and told Brown Bear that he would show him if he promised not to eat him.

Since the great bear had not listened to Beaver, and had made the mistake of killing all the other bears by destroying the dam, he listened to Ground-hog and promised not to harm smaller animals anymore.

So Ground-hog quickly shook his entire body and all the water flew from his fur, leaving him dry. Next, Brown Bear tried the same trick, but because he was so big and clumsy, it took him several tries. The bear was very thankful because now he could keep his skin on whenever he got wet.

"Where are you going to live now?" asked Ground-Hog.

The bear looked about and replied, "Among the rocks and boulders on this side of the peak."

"Good," said the ground-hog. "I will live on the other side of the mountain so that I will not get in your way."

And so the bear learned not to be too proud and boastful because he had not listened to Beaver and had killed his relatives, and because he had learned a good trick from the ground-hog.

Raven Made The Rivers, Lakes, And Streams
(How Raven Became Black)

This is the legend of a fascinating encounter between
Raven and Ganook, another Tlingit deity whose power we
learn was even greater than Raven's. The myth accounts
for the creation of the rivers, lakes and streams, and
also of how the raven came to be black.

In the very, very beginning Raven shared the world with
several other very powerful beings. The most powerful of all then
was Ganook, or The Sitting One.

Once, when Raven met Ganook while canoeing on the sea, Ganook,
wanting to show his power and superiority over Raven, took off
his magic hat and made a thick fog cover the entire sea. The fog
was so dense that Raven could not even see the front of his
canoe!

Ganook paddled his craft away from Raven, who was not black
then but white, and left him alone. Unable to see at all, Raven
wandered about the surface of he sea for a long time. Finally, he
became scared and yelled out into the fog, "Ganook! My
brother-in-law! Where are you?"

But Ganook kept quiet and patiently watched as Raven, his
brother-in-law, paddled every which way and became very lost.

Raven kept calling for Ganook imploring him to show himself
and to make the fog go away. Finally Ganook came up close to him
in his canoe.

"What is the matter, brother-in-law? Why do you cry so?" he
asked the relieved white raven.

Ganook placed his hat on his head and instantly the thick fog
lifted.

Raven looked at Ganook and said, "You are much stonger than I
am."

"How long have you been living in the world?" asked Ganook.

Raven answered that he was born before the world was even at
its present place. Then he asked Ganook how long he had lived in
the world.

The Sitting One answered, "Since the time when the liver has
come up from underneath."

Raven thought about this for a moment and said, "Yes, you are
older than I am."

After this Ganook invited Raven to his home, the island of
Deikee Noow. Together they ate a feast and Ganook offered the
white bird some fresh water. Raven had never drank this before

because there was only sea water in the world. Ganook had the only fesh water and he kept it in a giant stone well with a heavy stone lid.

Raven very much liked the taste of the water and wanted more but he was afraid to ask because Ganook was more powerful than he was. After the meal, Raven told stories about his origin and about the creation of the world. Ganook listened for a while but became tired and soon fell asleep on the great stone lid which safegaurded the fresh water.

When his brother-in-law was fast asleep, Raven took some dog excrement and placed it under Ganook. Having done this, he walked some distance away and called to Ganook.

"Wake up! Look at what you have done!" yelled Raven.

When he heard Raven's words, Ganook jumped up and saw the excrement. Thinking that he had messed himself, he ran to the sea to wash. Raven wasted no time. He ran to the well and lifted the great lid and drank some water. When he had quenched his thirst he filled his mouth with water. Then he started to fly up through the smokehole but Ganook stopped him.

Ganook built a fire and began to smoke the white raven for having tricked him. The smoke from the fire turned Raven black. This is how he became black. He had always been white before. Finally, though, Ganook took pity on his brother-in-law and let Raven go.

Raven flew away towards his home on the Nass River and as he flew, drops of the fresh water he stole fell from his beak. Wherever the drops of water landed lakes, rivers and springs appeared upon the land.

Chilkat Blanket

Like the Totem Pole itself, Chilkat blankets tell a story through their beautifully decorated weavings. This myth tells of their origin and how Raven eventually brought them to the Tlingit people.

A small group of Tlingit women went into the forest to gather wild celery. It was early spring and the celery would be good to eat after after a whole winter of eating nothing but dried salmon and oil. They collected as much wild celery as they could and tied it into bundles so that they could carry them to the village. late that day, they started homeward.

One of the women was the young daughter of the chief. She put some large bundles of celery on her back and walked with the others. Along the trail home were some nice dried branches and twigs and the chief's daughter decided to pick some for starting fires at home.

As she walked to the dried wood, she suddenly slipped and fell into a huge brown bear's footprint. Her bundle of wild celery broke open as she fell and was scattered all over. While gathering the food, she was all the while grumbling about how bad bears were. She said very bad things about all bears, everywhere in the world.

The other women kept walking down the trail carrying their bundles of wild celery on their backs.

Finally, the young woman had tied her bundle together with her leather thongs and was on her way home to join the others.

Presently, though, she heard footsteps behind her. She turned quickly to see who it was and found herself in the arms of a very handsome young man. He spoke gently and kindly to her and asked her to marry him. He was so handsome and strong that she agreed and they were soon walking deep into the dark forest on their way to his home. When they arrived at his village, the girl learned that he was of the Bear clan.

The young chief's daughter did not like living with the people of the Bear clan and so she ran away. When she reached the sea she saw a fisherman in a canoe, but he would not help her until she promised to marry him. She agreed and he came to shore. Just as she stepped into the canoe, her husband and the men of the Bear clan came out of the forest towards the craft.

The fisherman sprang at the Bear clan husband and hit him on the head with his killing club. The handsome young man instantly fell dead.

The young woman learned that her new husband was not a man at all, but a spirit named Gonaquade't. After killing the Bear clan husband, Gonaquade't shoved off the canoe and paddled out to sea. Soon the canoe sank to the bottom of the ocean where he lived in a rock house under the water.

When they reached the house, Gonaquade't wrapped his new wife in a cedar-bark mat and carried her through the rock house to a large room in the back.

They had a very happy life together and her new husband was very kind and gentle. Soon they had a son and he was just like any other boy.

When the son was old enough to learn how to hunt and fish, the wife asked Gonaquade't if she could move to her village where her uncle could teach the boy the ways of her people. Gonaquade't agreed as long as she promised not to forget him.

She agreed and kept her promise by weaving a beautiful blanket which had pictures showing how they met. It took a long time to make. When it was complete her son was already a man. The wife took the blanket to Gonaquade't's house under the sea.

One day, Raven went to visit Gonaquade't. When he entered the rock house, he saw the beautiful blanket Gonaquade't was now wearing over his shoulders.

They visited each other for a long time and ate a feast together. Afterwards, Gonaquade't taught Raven many dances which he could show his people. When it was time for Raven to go, Gonaquade't gave him the blanket because it was his most precious possession. Raven thanked him for the gift and took it to his people so that they could make blankets just like it.

Gonaquade't had the very first Chilkat blanket, but after Raven brought it to the people, there were many blankets-with-a-story. The people who make it call themselves the Chilkat, and they still use the blankets in their dances—the ones that Raven taught them.

Blackskin

One of the greatest Tlingit and Haida mythological characters is the young Blackskin, their equivalent of the Greek mythological hero, Hercules, and the Judeo-Christian hero, Samson. There exists numerous accounts of his heroic deeds.

A long time ago all of the men in a small village wanted to be very strong so that they could hunt sea lions better. So every morning the men would run down to the sea and jump into the freezing, cold water to bathe. This, it was thought, proved that they were strong.

Afterwards, they would all take turns trying to twist the giant tree in the center of the village. The strongest men would grab the trunk of the tree and twist with all of their might, but none could tear the tree from its roots.

The men of this village did many things so that they would become very, very strong.

The Chief of the village had a young nephew named Blackskin who would one day become chief. But the young man did not behave as a young chief-to-be should. He didn't try to show his strength by twisting the giant tree. He always slept during the day and did not bathe in the very cold sea water with the other young men of the village. He earned his name because he always slept too close to the fire and his skin was black from the soot.

All of the villagers laughed at the young man because he was so weak and lazy. His own family, especially his two brothers, were ashamed of him. His brothers always called him weakling and lazy.

But Blackskin was neither of these things. Instead, he went and bathed alone in the water at night when everyone was asleep and was becoming very strong. His uncle once noticed him leave the village at night and not come home until the next morning before everyone was awake. He knew that Blackskin was strong and could endure the icy cold water longer than any other man in the village.

Although the rest of the village still thought him to be weak coward, Blackskin was a good man. He did not fight and he did not lie. He helped gather wood for the elders and he kept their fires burning.

Each night when everyone was asleep he returned to the sea and bathed there alone in the cold water lit only by the pale moonlight. He grew stronger and stronger, but he did not want to tell anyone how strong he was growing.

One day a terrible hunting accident happened. A group of men had gone sea lion hunting and when they were fighting one large sea lion its tail hit the Chief and killed him. His body was brought back to the village where a funeral ceremony befitting a chief was given in his remembrance.

Many stories were told during the ceremony of great legendary heroes who held great honor in their village. Blackskin enjoyed these stories and never tired of hearing them. He hoped that he too would one day bring great honor to his people.

Once the eight day funeral ritual was over, the men of the village vowed to return and kill the sea lion who had killed the chief. But first they had to prepare for the hunt and train their bodies by enduring the cold water. They also hit one another with branches to learn to endure pain and to toughen the skin.

Fearing that the others would laugh at him as they always had, Blackskin did not join them. Instead, he decided to avenge his uncle's death alone because he was certain that the uncle had been proud of him. So, every night he continued to endure the cold sea water bathe alone.

His aunt noticed his secret and encouraged him to stay in the water longer and longer each night so that he would gradually build up his stength. Sometimes he would stay in the water so long that he could barely even crawl onto the shore. He switched himself with a branch harder and harder until his skin burned, but he endured the pain. He was becoming very strong indeed!

One night, when Blackskin was bathing alone, he saw a man wearing a bearskin walking on the beach. he had never seen the man before and asked who he was.

"I am called Strength," said the man. "I have come to help you."

The stranger told Blackskin to fight him to show how strong he was.

When the chief-to-be approached him, the man grabbed him, picked him up over his head, and threw him onto the sand. Blackskin looked up in amazement.

He wrestled with the bearskin-clad man several times, but each time he was defeated by the stranger.

"You are not strong enough yet," said Strength. "You must train more and then you will be ready to test your strength against the village tree. I will help you, but you must not tell anyone that you have seen me."

Back in the village, the other men would wrestle to train themselves, but whenever Blackskin wrestled he always let himself be beaten because he didn't want anyone to know of his great strength. Most of the time he would just sleep during the day since he was so tired from training alone all night.

Everyone kept making fun of him and calling him lazy and weak.

One night, when Blackskin was bathing in the cold sea, the small man called Strength returned and invited him to wrestle again. This time Blackskin threw him to the ground!

"You are strong!" exclaimed Strength. "Now you are ready to twist the giant tree."

So the small man led Blackskin through the dark to where the village tree grew. Blackskin hugged the tree's trunk with both arms and twisted it right out of the ground!

"Now," said Strength, "replace it in the ground as it was. You are ready to fight and kill the sea lion who killed your chief. You are stronger than the North Wind."

The next morning, the men of the village bathed as usual and then went to try the tree. Blackskin's oldest brother was first to try the tree and he twisted it out on the very first try.

All of the men shouted, "We are ready. Our training is complete, now we can go hunt the sea lion."

Blackskin smiled when he heard this. But he did not tell anyone that he had twisted the tree in the night.

The next day the men were preparing their long boat for the trip and only the strongest men who had been training were chosen to go on the hunt.

Although he was not chosen, Blackskin was determined to be the one to avenge his uncle's death and kill the sea lion. He went to the wife of his uncle and asked her for the ancestral weasel-spirit hat which brought honor to the clan. She gladly gave it to him and was proud that he had asked for it. The other men, especially the two brothers, had not thought to wear the hat of honor.

Blackskin cleaned himself and dressed in fresh clothes and then walked down the beach to where the men were preparing to leave for the hunt.

When the others saw him, they were surprised. No longer was Blackskin the dirty, sooty young man they had always teased. Instead, he stood tall and somewhat confident wearing clean clothes and the ancestral hat. But nonetheless, they did not agree to let him join them.

Laughing, they pushed the long boat from the shore and began to paddle away. But Blackskin held the boat and kept it from moving even though all the men paddled as hard as they could. Then Blackskin lifted the entire canoe with all of the men in it right out of the water onto the beach!

The men thought that the tide must have washed the boat ashore. Surely, they thought, Blackskin had not done this.

The young chief-to-be asked if he could at least be the one to bail the water out of the craft. Because Blackskin was, after all, the nephew of the dead chief, the men agreed he could go along.

The men looked at Blackskin as he stepped into the canoe and one asked him, "How many sea lions are you going to kill?"

Blackskin didn't say a word. He climbed in and sat down in the bottom of the boat and went to sleep.

Finally the hunters reached the island where the sea lions lived. As the canoe came up to the rocky shore, the oldest brother jumped out. Sea lions were all around him. He killed several small animals as he made his way to the big bull. When he reached the bull, the oldest brother tried to twist its head off as he had twisted the tree in the village, but the giant sea lion threw him off and smashed him against the rocks, killing him as it had killed the chief.

Then the other brother tried to kill the sea lion bull, but it killed him, too.

The other men became afraid and wanted to leave.

"If the bull had so easily killed the two brothers," they thought, "then it can kill us as well."

They pushed the canoe off the island and started to leave. But

Blackskin stood up in the canoe and spoke bravely as a chief speaks.

"Turn the canoe around and take it back to the island. I will kill the sea lion bull and avenge my brothers and uncle."

They had never before seen or heard him speak or act like this and they saw that he was sure and confident. They realized that a chief had spoken and so they turned around and returned to the island.

Blackskin stepped out of the boat and went after the great bull that had killed his uncle and brothers. He grabbed many smaller ones by their tails and picked them up and dashed their heads against the rocks. When he came to the big bull, he wrestled with it and then picked it up over his head and threw it to the ground as he had done to Strength. Then he twisted its head off and tore the dead sea lion in half with his bare hands!

The other men were impressed. They had never before seen such strength in a man.

When he had killed the bull, Blackskin collected all of the sea lions he had killed and filled the boat with their bodies. There was plenty of meat for the entire village! The men were amazed and scared and returned home vowing to never again say mean things about Blackskin.

The news of his strength and courage, and of the honor he had bestowed upon the village soon spread and Blackskin was made chief. Throughout his life, he accomplished many great things and always brought honor to his people. Also, he only used his great strength for good. He was truly a great man.

ESKIMO

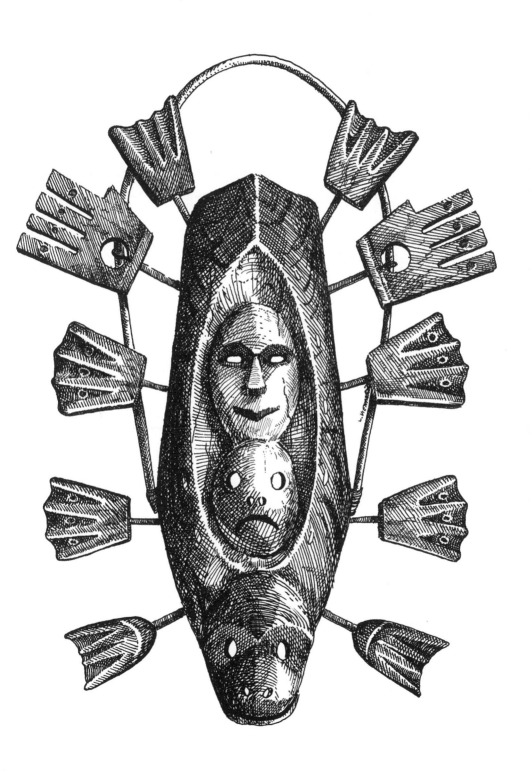

The Boy And The Bear

This is an amazing tale of adventure and danger when a young orphan becomes a great hunter after searching for hunters from his village, mysteriously lost while hunting caribou up river of their village.

Once there was a village near the mouth of a river. The men of the village were known as very good hunters. Their igloos were located in such a way that they could easily see the seals on the sea ice and the caribou migrating across the surrounding hills. Because of this, they were very successful hunters.

One day, though, a group of the men left the village on the river in search of caribou grazing in the hills. They used their kayaks and paddled many miles up the river. They did not return. After a while, a nother small group of hunters left to find the first group. They too never returned to the small village on the river by the sea.

The people remaining in the village began to grow concerned. They did not know what to do. If they sent more hunters up the river to find them, those men might be lost as well.

It so happened that in the village there lived a young boy whose parents had died when he was very young. Because he was an orphan, he was very poor and wished that he could someday have his own kayak and be a great hunter. When he learned that the two groups of hunters had disappeared, he decided that he would go in search of them alone. He asked the one of the older men in the village if he could borrow his spear and kayak so that he could find the lost men.

The old man warned him, "If you go up the river like the other hunters, there is a chance that you might never return. However, if you accept the risk then my kayak and spear are yours to use. They are both down at the river bank."

The boy wasted no time. He hurried down to the boat and quickly set out up the river. It was a long journey and so the boy hunted ducks and fish with the spear as he travelled. He practiced with the spear until his aim became very accurate. He was so good that he could kill birds flying overhead with a single throw of the long, thin spear.

After many days of paddling up the river, he saw some large igloos along the bank of the river ahead.

"That is most strange," he thought. "I have never heard of a village being this far up the river. Perhaps it is the camp of the lost hunters. Perhaps, though, they are prisoners here."

Since he was not certain who lived in the village, the boy approached the igloos cautiously. He pulled his kayak ashore far below the settlement and hid it where it would not be seen. Then he took his sharp spear and some of the dead birds and crept up to the closest igloo.

Looking around to make sure that no one saw him, the boy entered the igloo. Inside he was alone. He entered several other large igloos and they were all empty.

"If these are the houses of the lost hunters," he thought, "then they must be hunting presently."

He lay down to rest in the one of the deserted igloos while he waited for the men to return.

While resting, he heard something or someone approaching. Waiting quietly in a dark corner of the igloo, he watched the entrance and soon saw something coming through the hole. It was dark and all he could see was a mouth asking for something to eat. Without hesitation the boy threw one of the ducks that he had killed at the opening. The mouth greedily took the duck and disappeared.

The boy, still hiding in the corner, was frightened because he recognized the mouth as that of a bear-man. He had heard many horrible stories about these creatures who could take off their fur coats and lived in igloos like people. He remembered that they would kill and eat people who came upon their village. He knew that they were very dangerous.

A few minutes later the bear-man returned. Again, the boy threw one of his dead birds at the hungry, sharp-toothed mouth.

This continued for some time until the orphan realized that the bear-man had eaten all of his birds. The next time it came in the igloo it would eat him.

The boy was trapped. "This must be what happenend to the hunters from my village," he thought. "They must have come here and were eaten by the terrible bear-men, just as I am to be."

He was scared but he wanted to be a great hunter so he made a plan. When the bear-man stuck his head into the igloo asking for food this time, he would throw his spear at it.

The next time the bear-man entered, he took careful aim and threw his harpoon with all of his strength. The point went deep into the creature but did not immediately kill it. He tried to pull the spear out but it broke in two.

Realizing that he was in certain danger, the boy fled the igloo. He ran into a nearby igloo which was smaller than the first with out even listening to hear if anyone was home.

Inside were two old bear-women. Instantly he fell upon them with his skinning knife and killed them. He skinned one of them, and after hiding the body he wore the fur coat. The other he leaned against the igloo wall as if she were merely sleeping. When he had finished this, he heard someone approaching the entrance.

A large bear-man entered the small igloo and said, "The great hunter in the igloo next to yours has been attacked and there is a spear sticking in his body. He is suffering greatly. You must come and take care of his wound."

The boy wearing the woman's fur coat answered, "I can no longer walk. I am very tired and my companion has fallen asleep and I do not wish to wake her. She needs her rest."

But the bear-man insisted. "You must come. We will lift you up and carry you to the igloo. He will die if you do not help him."

The boy knew that he had to go, so he slowly rose to his feet and walked like a trembling old woman. The bear-man grabbed one of his arms and dragged him to the nearby igloo. Although the boy tried to act like an old bear-woman, he could not do so entirely.

The bear-man became suspicious.

"How is that you seem stronger than usual?" he asked.

The boy thought quickly. "It is because I am trying with all my strength to walk so that I can help my wounded brother."

The bear-man was satisfied and asked no more questions.

Inside the large igloo where he had hid earlier, the boy saw the bleeding bear-man lying on the floor with part of the spear's shaft protruding from his chest. He looked about the room and saw a large, sharp stone. He heated it over a oil lamp flame while telling the bear-man who had brought him what he was going to do.

"I am going to pull the harpoon from our brother, but first I must heat this stone so that I can place it upon the wound to stop the bleeding."

The bear-man nodded.

"When I am ready to remove the harpoon," he continued, "you must blow out the lamp and make a lot of noise. This is part of the healing and must be done."

The bear-man nodded again.

The boy began to work. First he grabbed the broken end of the spear and told the bear-man to begin. Once the room was pitch dark, the boy pulled the spear out and plunged the hot stone deep into the wound. The wounded bear-man howled in pain but the other bear-man could not see or hear because he was making a great deal of noise as instructed.

In a moment the bear-man was dead. The boy prepared to escape but before he did he thrust the harpoon into the heart of the other bear-man who was still busy making noise.

Quickly, the orphan boy pulled out the broken spear and ran as fast as he could to his kayak. He jumped in and paddled furiously down river.

The other villagers, having seen him running and having heard the screams of the two dead bear-men, chased the boat along the shore. They followed him for a long distance but were never able to get close enough to catch him. Finally, they gave up and went home.

When the boy returned to his village by the sea he told the story of his adventure. He showed the amazed hunters the bear skin and the bloody, broken harpoon and they knew what had happened to the two groups of lost hunters.

The older man who had loaned the orphan his kayak and spear was satisfied with what the boy had done and gave him the kayak and a new harpoon. From that time on the boy became a man and was known as a great hunter.

The Blind Boy And The Loon

This is a fairly common Alaskan Native legend which
appears in Yupik, Inupiaq, Upper Tanana, Tanaina, and
Eyak mythology. Although the stories are quite similar,
they naturally include very different settings. Whereas
the Eskimo version involves a big polar bear, the
athabaskan narratives involve a moose.

A blind Eskimo boy once lived with his mother in a house built
near the beach. The boy had become blind as a young boy when the
wicked and cruel mother rubbed dirt in his eys while he was
sleeping, and the mother supported them by gathering roots and
berries in the summer. She also walked along the beach looking
for dead seals, walrus, or whales which might have washed ashore.
These she cleaned as best she could and preserved them so that
they would have meat during the long winter. In this way, they
were able to survive.

It was very difficult for the old woman to support her son.
She had to travel to the larger villages to beg for supplies such
as clothes and oil for their cooking stove. Sometimes she would
go fishing on the ice when there was no other food for them to
eat.

One day while they were sitting in their igloo, they heard
something walking in the snow outside the igloo. It circled
around the house and then climbed on top and looked into the
skylight hole. The old woman saw that it was a large polar bear.
She was terrified. Then it stuck its great paw through the hole
and tried to reach them.

The old woman grabbed the son's bow and arrows and gave it to
him. Desperately, he tried to notch the arrow and then pulled
back with all his strength. The mother directed Ahyonhgarouk so
that he was pointing directly at the bear. When he let go the
arrow struck the bear in a vital place. The polar bear died
almost instantly without making a sound. But the old lady said to
her blind son, "You missed it."

Of course Ahyonhgarouk did not know what had happened.

Afterwards, the old woman told her son that she had to go out
and fix the skylight. She took her ulu and repaired the damage
quickly and then skinned the bear and cut up the meat and hid it.
She scraped all of the fat off the skin and hung it up to dry.

While she was still outside, she cooked some of the meat and
ate it without sharing with her blind son. When she was finished
feeding herself, she cooked some scraps of the old meat she found

on the beach and gave it to her son. As he ate the little bit of food, the old woman scolded Ahyonhgarouk for having missed the bear. The greedy woman knew that he had not missed it, but she wanted to keep all of the meat for herself. There was more than enough food for the whole winter but she wasn't going to share with her poor blind son.

Then it became springtime and all of the snow melted. The tundra was turning green and the small birds were singing and flying everywhere. Ahyonhgarouk listened to the birds and knew that there was a small lake behind the house where they were making nests. He wished that he could see the beauty of the world around him but all he could do was listen.

As he listened he heard a loon. He knew that the sound came from the lake but it sounded different. It seemed to him as if the loon was actually speaking. Ahyonhgarouk listened very carefully and when the bird made another sound he was certain that it was talking and calling to him.

The blind boy could hear his mother sleeping and so he crawled out of the house and felt his way towards the loon's voice. He was getting closer and closer to the loon and he could hear it splashing in the water. When he got to the edge of the lake he stopped and the loon swam to him.

"I have been watching you and want to help you." said the loon. "You never harmed or molested my young ones when you were hunting. I want to help you if I can, so you must do as I say. Get on my back and hang on tight and don't let go. I will dive with you on my back."

So the giant loon swam out to the deep part of the lake with Ahyonhgarouk on its back and dived four times. Each time the blind man held his breath. When the loon came up the fourth time it told Ahyonhgarouk to open his eyes.

He did and to his surprise he could see! He thanked the loon and when he returned to his home, he saw the polar bear skin and the meat and he knew that his mother had lied to him about the polar bear, and that she had eaten the meat and gave him only old scraps, trying to slowly starve him.

Ahyonhgarouk went inside the house and saw that his bed and blanket was filthy. There was dirt and bugs all over his clothes and blanket, and his drinking water was filled with lice! He was very angry that his mother had mistreated him so badly.

He woke his mother and said that he was hungry. Ahyonhgarouk pretended to still be blind and when she brought him a bowl with only a few berries and some fat, he threw it down and told her that he could see now. He told her how the loon had helped him and how he knew that he had killed the polar bear. The wicked, greedy mother was frightened and tried to escape.

The boy grabbed her and took her whale hunting in their umiak. When Ahyonhgarouk saw a large white whale, he threw his harpoon into its back and then quickly tied the end of the harpoon rope to his greedy mother's waist. It pulled her into the icy water and beneath the surface.

Whenever Ahyonhgarouk went seal hunting after that, he sometimes saw his mother still tied to the back of the whale and he felt sorry for her because she had been so unkind and greedy.

The Ten-Footed Polar Bear

The story of the Ten-Footed Polar Bear, although very interesting, is also quite rare. Throughout all of my research and years of collecting Eskimo legends, I have come across only two recordings of this unique tale.

Along the nothern coast of Alaska, there once lived a Ten-Footed Polar Bear. It spent much of its time in the water swimming between icebergs off the ice pack hunting seals and so it was rarely seen by Eskimos. No one knows why it had ten feet instead of four like all other bears, but it did. It had five feet on each side and when it walked or ran all five feet on one side moved forward and then the other side followed.

Because he had so many legs, when the Ten-Footed Polar Bear ran, he would sometimes get his feet all tangled up and then he would fall down. This is why he spent so much time in the water, because he was not so clumsy.

A long time back, before there was white men in the arctic, a great Eskimo hunter was hunting seal on the ice pack. He had killed a seal and was dragging it a long distance across the frozen landscape on his journey home to his village.

All of a sudden he came upon a strange sight. In the snow was the track of a polar bear, or many polar bears. He could not be sure. He had heard the strange stories of a Ten-Footed Polar Bear which hunted far away from the villages and was rarely seen by Eskimos, but he didn't believe there was such a bear.

He continued on his way still pulling the dead seal with one arm while the other held his long spear. Then the man heard the ten feet of the Ten-Footed Bear making tracks in the snow just behind him. He stopped and looked over his shoulder. Coming over a tall snowdrift close by, was the polar bear. The hunter was frightened. He had never seen a Ten-Footed Polar Bear and he didn't know what to do!

Quickly, he released the dead seal and ran, still holding his long spear. The great bear ran after him with his ten heavy paws barely sinking in the snow. It stopped for a minute and ate the seal, but then followed after the scared hunter.

The man saw two big blocks of ice close together. He ran towards them and hid there. But the Ten-Footed Bear smelled his scent and ran straight at him, tripping over his clumsy feet on the way.

The wind was blowing the snow all over and for a moment the man could not see the bear, nor could the bear see the man. The hungry polar bear climbed on top of the ice and fell in between the two ice blocks. It landed upside down and got its feet all tangled up when it tried to get up.

The Eskimo hunter took his heavy spear and threw it with all of his strength and hit the Ten-Footed Bear in the heart. Its ten great feet waved back and forth in the air as it desperately tried to get up. But soon it was dead.

The hunter cut off all ten of the bear's feet and took them to his village, but no one believed that he had killed the Ten-Footed Polar Bear. Since that time, though, no one has ever seen such a strange and mysterious polar bear in the arctic.

Raven And Owl

There are several Tlingit myths which explain how Raven became black. It is said that the great bird was white at the very beginning. The following is an Eskimo legend of how Raven became black.

Once Raven was very white like the snow on the tundra and so was Owl. One day, while sitting on a rock looking for rabbits, Raven flew down and landed beside the white owl.

They had known each other for a very long time and were always challenging one another to see which was the strongest. Raven sat down on the rock next to his old friend.

"Let's wrestle," said Raven.

"I do not want to fight you today," answered Owl.

But the white raven did not listen.

"Let's wrestle," he repeated.

"I do not want to wrestle. I do not feel like it today," replied the white owl.

But Raven still would not listen and started to wrestle with the unwilling Owl.

They rolled around the ground and when Owl saw a mud puddle, he pushed Raven into it. The black mud covered his entire body. No white remained at all! Raven was very mad because he was so muddy and because Owl had pushed him in.

"Friend Owl," said the mischievous bird, "give me a hand so that I can get out of this mud hole."

But the white owl was wise to Raven's tricks and deceits.

"No." he said. "You are the one who started the fight. I said that I didn't want to wrestle today."

Raven thought for a minute and then said, "Friend, if you help me out I will give you half of my possessions."

So Owl reached down and pulled Raven out of the thick, black mud. Raven was still covered from head to foot and he was no longer white like the snow.

As soon as he was out, the black bird shook his feathers and mud flew all over the place. Some of it splattered on Owl's white feathers, leaving him spotted with small black specks.

To this day ravens are entirely black and owls are spotted.

Fox And Raven

Just as the previous story found Raven and Owl wrestling in a mud hole, this story finds Raven tricking Fox in a similar account.

Raven always thought that he was the smartest in the world. But Fox thought that he was pretty smart, too. Neither of the two liked the other very much, but they held each other in some respect and always acted like friends, even if they weren't.

As with his friend Owl, Raven was always trying to better Fox. One winter day he went to Fox and said, "Friend Fox, won't you come and play with me?"

Fox looked at Raven and asked him what he wanted to do.

"Let's play slide-down-the-hill," was the black bird's reply.

Now Fox was proud and didn't want Raven to know that he didn't want to play with him. You see, if Raven knew that Fox didn't want to play, then Raven might think that he was afraid of him or that he was unable to beat him in a game.

"Friend Raven," replied Fox, "I would like to play with you."

Raven laughed to himself because he was going to trick his friend. He laughed because at the very bottom of the hill was a wide mud puddle which hadn't quite frozen yet.

But Fox wasn't stupid. He knew all about the mud pond at the bottom of the hill, but he wasn't going to say anything about it.

Instead, he followed Raven to the top of the hill and when they were at the very top, Fox looked over the side and invited Raven to go first.

"You thought of the game," he said. "You should be the first to slide down the hill."

Raven thought carefully. He didn't want to let Fox know about the mud pond, but he knew that he had to accept the invitation or Fox would become suspicious.

"Very well, Friend Fox," he said. "I will go first and have fun sliding down the hill."

With that, Raven slid down the long hill going faster and faster until he was almost to the bottom where the mud was. He was going so fast that he could not stop, but he didn't want to. He just spread his wings a little and gently flew over the mud puddle without getting any dirt on himself whatsoever. From the great height of the hilltop, Fox could not easily see that Raven had flown over the mud pond.

Raven stopped on the other side of the puddle and turned facing up the hill at Fox.

"It is your turn now, friend Fox, yelled Raven. "Let me see you slide down the hill as I just did."

"Oh, no," replied Fox. "I know that there is a wide mud puddle at the bottom and that I will fall into it."

"But you can jump over it at the last moment and then you will not be muddy," responded the mischievous black bird.

Fox stood alone for a minute with the wind blowing through his soft white fur staring at the bottom of the hill. He knew that he must slide down or else Raven would think that he was smarter and better than he was. He thought that if Raven had jumped over it, then he could too.

So Fox started sliding down the hill. Faster and faster he went until he was sliding even faster than Raven had. When he came to the bottom of the hill, he saw the wide, unfrozen mud pond and gave a giant leap just before he landed in it. The puddle was wider than it looked and he landed right in the middle!

Raven laughed and laughed and said that he had never seen anything so funny.

Fox crawled out of the mud and stood on the puddle's edge.

Raven laughed even louder than before saying how he had tricked him and how much smarter than the fox he was.

Fox ran away to his home to clean himself. Since that time when Raven tricked Fox, they have never been friends again.

The Hunter And The Eagle

This myth, like most others, is didactic and yet at the
same time it explains the origin of white foxes in the
Eskimo arctic.

There once was a man who was a great hunter. Although he
always returned from hunts with food, he never killed anything
just for the fun of it. He had never harmed an animal for the
pleasure of killing it. He would not even harm a small bird or
insect unless he was going to eat it. This is the way all hunters
should be.

One day, a large eagle landed near him and the hunter killed
it with his spear. He took it to his camp and carefully cleaned
it. He saved the downy feathers and when he ate the meat he
didn't waste a single bite.

Later, when he was leaving his igloo, two large eagles landed
nearby. As he prepared to shoot them with his bow and arrow, one
of them took his headpiece off. It had a man's face!

Then the one spoke to him. "Our mother has sent us to get you
and take you to her. We shall both carry you and when she has
finished speaking with you, we will return you."

The hunter agreed. Since the two birds were quite large, he
was able to hang onto their feathers. Every now and then he had
to switch to ride on the other eagle because they became tired
from carrying him on the long journey to their mother's house.

They flew for a long time but finally arrived in a strange
land. As the hunter climed down from the great bird, an
eagle-woman greeted him with a smile. It was their mother.

She spoke to the hunter. "I thank you for showing respect for
my dead son. You did not waste any part of his body and you even
burned his bones. You kept his plumage intact and dried it so
that it hangs in your igloo. I thank you for giving him such
respect and wish to give you a gift. Look around my house and
take whatever you wish."

The eagle-woman showed him the many rooms of her house and
reminded him that he could have any one of her belongings as a
present. But the hunter was not sure that she was not going to
kill him. After all, he thought, he had killed her son with his
spear.

"Choose what you like and my two sons will help carry it back
when they take you home," insisted the eagle-woman.

When the woman showed him a room with white foxes in it, the
hunter said that he wanted some of them. The woman was glad that

66

he had accepted her gift. She took some of the white foxes and cut off small pieces of their ears which she placed in a skin bag. Then she gave the bag to the hunter to wear around his neck and told her two sons to return him to his home.

Just before they left, though, the eagle-woman told the hunter that her sons were going to take him close to his home, but that he would still have to walk some distance to reach his igloo.

"If you become thirsty on the walk," she said, "be careful that you close your eyes when you bend down to take a drink."

The two brothers flew away with the hunter and his gift. After a long time they landed and left him where he was within a short walking distance to his own village. As soon as they left, the man set out for his home with the skin bag still around his neck.

As he walked, he became thirsty. When he stopped to drink, he forgot about the eagle-woman's advice. He bent low over the water and drank with his eyes open!

Just then the skin bag inflated like a balloon and burst open. All of the small pieces of ears cut from the white foxes went flying all over the ground, and as they landed in the snow, they turned into real living foxes and ran away. The man chased a few but they got away. This is how white foxes came to be, because eagle-woman gave them as a gift to the Eskimo.

Crane And Goose

Eskimo men, like those of other parts of the world, often test their strength against other men. One of their games of strength is a contest in which two men, who have tied a loop of string around their ear, pull against an opponent until one can no longer bear the pain and loses. This short story depicts Crane and Goose in a very similar contest.

A goose was walking along the shore of a small lake looking for something good to eat. He found a place where nice plants grew and decided to stop and eat them.

Soon a female crane flew overhead and saw him sitting among the tasty plants. She began circling him trying to attract his attention. She flew high in the air and then dived and danced while in flight.

The goose watched her and said, "You certainly must be tired. Come and rest here beside me and keep me company for I am all alone. Perhaps we could play a game."

"What shall we do?" asked Crane. "Shall we dance together?"

Goose answered saying that he was a terrible dancer.

"However," he said, "we can play a strength game. We can pull each other's neck and see who is the strongest."

The crane agreed and she landed beside the goose.

The two birds faced one another and entwined their long, thin necks and started to pull. Slowly, the crane pulled her opponent's neck toward the ground.

Goose saw that he was losing and so gave one great pull to win, but he soon became tired and fell down.

He jumped to his feet and faced the crane who now began to sing her victory song which greatly insulted Goose.

When she finished her song, the goose began to sing his own song which told of how his webbed feet were better than hers for swimming.

Just then a flock of crane were flying overhead.

Crane stopped Goose's singing.

"Listen!" she said. "Here comes my family. They will want to see us dance. Please dance with me so that I can honor them."

But Goose insisted that he could not dance and so Crane joined the flying birds without a gift because Goose would not dance.

The Boy Who Couldn't Remember

I have found several variations of this strange tale. Edward Keithahn's and Emily Ivanoff Brown's versions seem to be the most closely related and so I present a version resembling their retellings.

A long time ago a young Eskimo boy lived alone with his grandmother in a small village at the edge of the sea. In the winter, the old grandmother would send the boy ice fishing so that they could have food.

The boy would take his fishing equipment and walk out upon the ice until he found a place where he knew that fish had been caught by others. Then he would build a low ice shelter to block the ferocious wind and make a hole in the ice to fish. He would fish until he caught enough for his grandmother and himself. Then he would go home to eat them.

One day when he was ice fishing, he lay down on the ice and looked through the dark hole. Just below the surface a tomcod swam up and looked at him.

"What is your name?" the boy asked the fish.

The tomcod replied, "My name is Ayagghsra."

The boy couldn't believe it, the fish had actually spoken to him in his own language! He decided to run home to tell his grandmother what had happened. Grabbing his bag of fish and equipment, he started for the distant village, repeating the fish's name so that he would not forget it.

But before he had gone very far, the boy forgot the name and walked back to the hole and looked through it again.

"What is your name, fish? I have forgotten it," he said.

The fish again spoke to the boy, "I am Ayagghsra, the tomcod."

The boy thanked the fish once more and ran home as fast as he could, again repeating the name so that he would not forget it. But he stumbled and fell several times and when he was finally half way home he had forgotten the name again!

Angry that he could not recall a simple fish's name, he returned to the place and again asked the tomcod its name. It repeated its name and told the Eskimo boy not to run so fast. That way he wouldn't fall and forget this time.

All that time it was getting late and the ferocious wind was making it very cold. The boy was tired from walking back to the hole so many times. This time, though, he walked slowly and repeated the name aloud over and over again.

"Ayagghsra, Ayagghsra, Ayagghsra," he said to himself.

It was very cold and his breath had frozen to his parka hood. The sweat, from running before, was freezing to his body.

This time he reached the very door to his house, but just as he was about to walk in, he forgot the fish's name again! He was determined not to quit. As tired and cold as he was, he decided to return to the hole in the ice out upon the frozen sea. But no sooner did he begin to take a step then he fell dead at his grandmother's door.

Taboo Story

Every Alaskan native group, indeed most subsistence cultures world-wide, have rules or societal taboos regarding the respect of the animals, birds, and fish which are hunted for survival. As a boy, my father, an Alaskan native himself, always taught me to properly care for game animals. This Eskimo tale describes the punishment for breaking this very important rule.

When young boys are trained to fish and hunt, one of the first lessons they are taught is to respect and care for the animals they hunt. If animals are mistreated, then they may no longer allow themselves to be killed for food and clothing and the Eskimos would die of starvation or freeze to death. Therefore, fathers always tell their children to show respect when they kill for food.

One day, though, two young brothers were sent from their village to check on their ptarmigan snares. As they approached the traps, they saw one white ptarmigan caught by the leg in one of the snares. The bird was frightened and tried desperately to escape. It jumped up and down and tried to fly away, but the snare was very tight around its leg and it could not get away.

The brothers watched the bird and then one of them spoke to the other.

"I wonder if ptarmigan can fly straight without eyes?" he said smiling.

The other brother laughed and grabbed the bird and poked its eyes out with a small branch. Then he threw the blind bird into the air and it tried to fly, but it could not see if it was flying up or down. It kept crashing into the hillside and into small trees. The two brothers chased it while laughing aloud.

Then the other brother said, "I wonder if ptarmigan can fly without feathers?"

The younger brother grabbed the blind bird and began to pluck the feathers while the bird was still alive! When he was finished, he threw it into the air but each time it just fell to the ground. They did this for some time until it was time to inspect the other traps. They dropped the poor bird and walked away, leaving it to die. They did not even take its meat for food!

The next morning, both boys awoke in their parent's house feeling very sick. They had the fever and they kept throwing up. The shaman was sent for but he could do nothing for them. He made great spells and gave them special medicine made of herbs, but nothing relieved the pain and suffering of the two boys. Soon, blood began to pour from their eyes!

The shaman spoke to the father and mother and said that the sickness was too great. He said that they must have broken a taboo.

That very night, the two boys who had shown such great disrespect for the ptarmigan died in agony.

The Mammoth Hunters

In the not so distant past, giant woolly mammoths roamed the Alaskan tundra. Periodically, remains are found and restored by paleontologists. Eskimos, however, have long known of these creature's existence, and their mysticism permeates their mythology. This Inupiaq Eskimo legend involves the sighting of a mammoth and a ghostly band of hunters who can only be seen by shamans.

One time, near the Kobuk River, an Eskimo man named Ataogoraachuak was out hunting marmots, fat squirrel like animals that live in the arctic. He had killed two marmots up in the hills and had eaten both of them for his lunch.

Later that afternoon, the weather turned bad. Fog rolled in and covered the hilltops and filled the valleys below so thick that Ataogoraachuak could barely see. He stayed on the trail along the mountainside, and when he looked down the creek which ran beside the trail, he saw the vague outline of some large animal walking along, as though it were floating in the air.

The hunter tried to follow the ghostly animal but there were no tracks to follow. He could barely see the image ahead when suddenly three men appeared before him following the great beast. The men had long spears and were themselves floating in the air.

Two of the strange men approached the hunter and said, "Our brother will catch the mammoth and kill it."

Then the other invited Ataogoraachuak to follow them and help cut up the mammoth's carcass. But the Eskimo was truly frightened. He had never before seen a woolly mammoth, even though he had heard stories about them when he was young.

Then the first man said to him, "If you will help us, then you will become a great shaman. You will be able to know when it will snow, and when spring will come, and where the polar bears hole up."

Finally Ataogoraachuak agreed and followed the two strange men whose feet did not touch the ground. They walked together a short distance and came upon the third strange man and the dead mammoth. The three hunters told the Eskimo to build a fire so they could cook the meat for dinner. Once the fire was built, Ataogoraachuak used his knife to help cut the mammoth's meat.

The four hunters ate together and when all of the meat was cut and placed in their packs, the three strangers told the Eskimo to go home, but they instructed him to turn around once he had walked a short distance from the campfire.

So Ataogoraachuak started home, and after walking only a few steps, looked back at the place he had been. The mammoth's body was gone and the three hunters, with packsacks full of meat, were walking up into the sky. The astonished Eskimo watched as the three ghosts finally vanished in the air!

When Ataogoraachuak reached home, he told his people the story and they said that he had seen the ghost of long dead shamans who had hunted mammoths when they were alive. From that time on, Ataogoraachuak was a great shaman and seer because of his adventure.

How Crane's Eyes Became Blue

This wonderful Yupik Eskimo tale about Crane is reminiscent of the Western didactic story of "The Boy Who Cried Wolf."

A long time ago, on a small lake near where Bethel is today, there lived a crane.

One morning Crane was flying just over the tree tops looking for berries to eat. As he flew along the Kuskokwim River, he eventually found a wonderful patch of berries growing along the riverbank. He landed amidst the patch and saw how many delicious and juicy berries were growing there.

So, Crane took out his two eyes and placed them on a nearby tree stump and told them to watch out for predators which might try to eat him while he was busy eating the berries.

He was eating the delicious berries when all of a sudden his eyes yelled at him, "Something is coming! Something is coming!"

Crane quickly groped for his eyes and put them back into their place. But he saw nothing coming.

"Eyes, you must not fool me while I am eating," he said as he placed them back where they had sat along the riverbank.

He had no sooner began to eat again when his eyes screamed, "Hurry, something is coming to get you!"

But after Crane had put his eyes back in, he saw nothing. He was growing angry and said, "Do not trick me again, eyes."

Crane replaced the eyes upon the tree stump on the river's edge and continued his feast.

Shortly thereafter the eyes yelled to him again, "Something is coming! Something is coming!"

This time Crane was not so easily tricked. Instead of being made a fool of again, he ignored the warning. He heard a noise nearby and when he asked the eyes about it, he heard only the fading words of the eyes saying, "Help, I am being carried off!"

Crane felt around for his eyes but could not find them. Something, or someone had carried them off. The blind bird picked up two cranberries to use for eyes, but they made everything look red. Next, he placed two blackberries in his eye sockets, but they made everything black as night.

"These will never do," he said as he searched for other berries to use.

Finally, he found two blueberries and used them for eyes. They worked well and made the sky and the river a pretty blue. Crane kept the new eyes and since then all cranes have blue eyes.

77

Walrus' Gift

Most legends and myths instruct or explain nature. This
warm-hearted tale does both: it shows the true spirit
of giving, and it explains the mytho-origin of two
natural phenomena.

A very long time ago, walruses could not float. They always
had to swim, which made them become very tired.

One day, a particularly large walrus was swimming towards
Walrus Island. But when he was still a long ways away, he became
so tired that he could not swim any longer.

"Why can't I float like a whale?" he thought to himself.

He stopped swimming so that he could rest, but each time he
did he began to sink because he could not float. The poor, fat
walrus had to keep swimming even though he was so very tired from
his long journey.

Finally, he came upon Walrus Island and slowly pulled himself
upon the rocky beach. He was so exhausted that he just lay at the
water's edge, feeling the cool water crashing upon his body. He
only wanted to sleep.

Just then, a ptarmigan, who had seen the walrus fighting to
keep afloat upon the rough sea, walked closer to the fat animal
lying upon the beach. The walrus saw the small bird coming but he
was too tired to care and only wanted to sleep. He did not wish
to speak with anyone.

"What are you doing?" asked the ptarmigan when she was close
enough to speak.

Walrus rolled over trying to ignore the bothersome bird.

"I saw you swimming." said Ptarmigan. "You were obviously very
tired and had great difficulty reaching this island."

The bird walked around to speak at Walrus' face and said,
"Wouldn't you much rather sleep in the water where bears could
not surprise you in your sleep?"

"Yes, of course." answered the heavy, tusked walrus. "I would
very much like to sleep on the water, but I cannot stay afloat."

Ptarmigan thought about the problem for a minute and then
spoke again, "Walrus, you may have my crop. It is full of air and
it will help you keep afloat so that you can sleep on the sea."

Walrus agreed and so the bird cut his neck open just below the
chin and placed her crop inside and then sewed the slit closed.
Walrus tried the new addition to his body and it worked! He could
float very easily now. He was very thankful for the gift and
asked Ptarmigan if she would accept a present.

"What can I give you in return for your wonderful gift?" he asked the kind bird.

Ptarmigan scratched her head and answered, "It is very hard for me to dig my house in the snow because I do not have claws on my feet."

"Very well," said Walrus as he removed some of his claws and gave them to his new friend.

Since that time, walruses can float and ptarmigan have sharp claws so that they can dig in the snow.

Arnarr, The Bear Woman

This Central Yupik story was translated and told to me by a native from Nunivak Island. Like several other Eskimo legends, this tale teaches the value of faithfulness in marriage and what the consequences of adultery might be when magic is invoked.

There once lived a hunter named Aacurrlii who lived with his wife, Arnarr, and their daughter, Arnaryar, in Nunarparmiut. Although Aacurrlii went seal hunting almost every day, he rarely seemed to bring home any meat. He would go out on the water for many days but he never seemed to kill a seal, even though bloodstains could sometimes be found in his kayak.

One day he left the village to go hunting and he never returned. His wife and daughter were very sad and they watched the sea for a long time hoping that Aacurrlii would return safely. Finally, though, they gave up hope and stopped looking for him.

After many months, a snowbird came to Aacurrlii's sodhouse where only Arnarr and Arnaryar now lived alone. When the wife went outside, the small snowbird started singing and told her that Aacurrlii was living on the other side of the mountain in another village.

"There," the bird told her, "he has two wives."

Arnarr was angry and when the bird finished its story, she thanked it and began to ready herself to travel to the other village. She put on wolf clothing and told her daughter not to be afraid of her when she returned. Then she told Arnaryar to hit her on the nose when she returned from the other side of the mountain.

"That way," she said, "I will not harm you."

Dressed as a wolf, Arnarr journeyed across the tundra and over the mountain top and finally came upon a sodhouse which had smoke coming from its skywindow. She looked into the house and then carefully entered it after removing all of her wolf clothing.

Inside, she found two women tending two large boiling kettles which sat upon a large stack of firewood. When the two women saw Arnarr, they did not know who she was or that she was Aacurrlii's wife. They saw the tattoo on Arnarr's face and the elder one asked her how she got such a pretty tattoo.

Thinking quickly, Arnarr answered, "You can get a wonderful tattoo like mine by putting your head under boiling water."

The elder woman was very excited, and although the younger woman was reluctant at first, she finally agreed to try it. So Arnarr held both of the women's heads in the boiling water until they died!

Afterwards, she placed the older woman's body near the storage area which was made of rocks, as if she were merely bending over to pick up some seal meat. She put the other woman's body up on the sodhouse roof, as if she were preparing to replace the skylight window. When she was finished, Arnarr tied two cutting boards onto her hips and a large wooden bowl onto her buttocks and then put on a bearskin and hid to wait for Aarcurrlii to return from seal hunting.

When the hunter arrived, he pulled his kayak out of the water and called to his two wives to come help him. Aacurrlii became angry when neither of the two women responded and so he walked towards the house with an oar in his hand. He called up to the woman on the sodhouse roof and when she did not answer, he gave her a slight shove with the oar and she fell off the roof, dead. Then he walked into the house where the other woman was bent over the seal meat and when he touched her with the oar, she fell over dead as well.

Arnarr, who had been watching, suddenly turned into a bear and attacked her unfaithful husband, killing him and ripping him into pieces! Then she went on a rampage and killed everyone in the small village. When she was done, she travelled back to Nunarparmiut where Arnaryar was watching for her. When she saw the large, ferocious bear approaching, Arnaryar forgot her mother's instructions and hid in their sodhouse.

Frustrated, Arnarr fought the residents of her own village and killed everyone, including her daughter. Then she left the village and wandered in the mountains where she lived until some hunters found her and killed her. When they skinned the bear, they found a dead woman inside with two cutting boards and a wooden bowl tied to her body. They knew that the bear was Arnarr.

The Woman Who Married The Muskrat

This Eskimo narrative from Chevak, like many Alaskan native legends, involves an animal who becomes a man and takes a human wife under the condition that she respects certain rules which hides his true identity.

Long ago there was a great hunter who lived in a village on the banks of a river just inland from the sea. He had a very beautiful daughter, and although all of the bachelor men in the village asked if they could marry her, the hunter never gave permission to any of them. Many men asked, but none were ever permitted her hand in marriage.

One day, though, a very handsome man asked if he could take her as his wife. The young woman knew of the young man and wanted very much to marry him. But the father did not permit him to take her as his wife. The daughter was so angry that she vowed never to take a husband.

After a year, even her father tried to talk her into marrying someone. But the woman was still angry because the father had sent away the only man she ever wanted to marry. Although many men asked to make her their wife, the woman would have none of them.

One day the woman was walking beside the oxbow lake just outside the village when she saw some young boys chasing something along the edge of the water. She came closer to see what it was and saw that it was a muskrat. The poor animal was scared and very tired from being chased by the boys. Although it tried to escape, it could no longer swim well and it appeared as if it would soon die.

The beautiful, unmarried woman told the boys to leave the muskrat alone and so they left it lying on the grass, near dead from exhaustion. The woman walked back to her house as well.

Several weeks later, a very handsome young man approached the woman while she was doing her chores. He was wearing a parka made of muskrat. He told her that he was from a nearby village and asked her to marry him.

There was something almost magical about the mysterious, strange man, but she agreed to marry him and soon they were husband and wife. The man was a good hunter and provided well for his wife. He always caught a lot of game and bearded seal and he was kind to her as well.

They lived together and were happy. The man had always warned that she must never take off his clothes or boots and dry them by the fire, even if they were wet.

Once, after a long hunting trip, the husband came home all wet. When he went to bed, the wife dried his very wet clothes and boots by the fire. When he awoke, he put on his clothes and boots which were now dry. He looked very surprised and after looking at his disobedient wife, he quickly ran from the house.

The wife ran after him, begging him to stop. She followed her husband to the very oxbow lake where the young boys had been chasing the muskrat. When the man reached the lake, he immediately dove in. The woman dove in right behind him and when they both came up together, they had turned into muskrats!

The woman had disobeyed his only rule and had dried his boots by the fire. Because of that, they were now muskrats and they lived in the lake for the rest of their lives as such.

The Giant Sea Monster

It seems that almost every cultural group living on or near the ocean has stories of sea monsters. I have heard of and seen several accounts of this Eskimo tale, and although there are some variations, mostly involving the creature's physical description, the stories are generally very similar.

A very long time ago, even before the oldest living Eskimo's grandfather's grandfather was born, a giant and terrible sea monster lived in the sea just off the coast at Wales.

The sea serpent was very long and green. It had many small legs like a caterpillar and two long antennae which grew upon its head and were so long that they could reach out of the sea and grab unsuspecting Eskimos from their sodhouses.

From time to time, it is said, the giant creature came out of the sea to eat people. The only escape, if it came to the village, was to run for the hills. Those caught by the monster were either eaten or drowned.

Whenever the inhabitants of Wales planned a seal or whale hunting trip, they would first climb the surrounding hills and watch the ocean's surface to see if it was calm and if the seals and small whales acted as if they were afraid of something terrible under the water. If the ugruk or whales acted strangely, then they knew that the sea serpent must be near and so the villagers ran for the hills. If there was no sign of the creature, then the men went hunting in their kayaks or umiaks, but they always feared the surprise return of the sea monster.

One day the sea serpent came to the village unexpectedly and its two long antennae slithered from beneath the water like two giant snakes and reached out and grabbed two old people who were near the beach. They screamed as they were pulled towards the icy water and the sea serpent roared loudly.

The villagers heard the terrible noise and ran for the hills. Parents had their children in their arms and the younger couples helped the elders to escape. But before everyone could reach the safety of the hills, several people had been captured and eaten by the monster.

A powerful shaman decided to use his magic upon the sea ssrpent and so took his drum and began beating on it. The creature backed away from the beach and dove beneath the water. The shaman ran along the beach in the very direction the creature was swimming, beating his drum all the while. As he ran, he sang a song to the serpent asking it to leave the village alone and to stop eating people.

The shaman followed the serpent's wake for a long time, always running along the beach singing and beating on his drum.

Finally, after coming upon a steep cliff, he looked over the side and saw the giant monster looking up at him! The man was scared, but he sang his song to the creature even louder as he danced and beat on his drum using all of his great magical powers. He told the sea serpent to stay away from his village and to stop eating Eskimos.

The monster listened and then sank away beneath the surface and swam away. It never again returned to Wales.

Caribou Man

This longer Eskimo narrative is the story of a hunter, discontented with life as a man, who leaves his family in search of a better life as another animal. In the end, though, he returns to find happiness where it had been all along.

There once was a man who lived with his wife, two children, and his wife's mother. They all lived in an igloo in a small village along on the edge of the sea. The man was a fair hunter and a good husband and father, but the mother-in-law was always saying how bad he was. At night, when she thought he was asleep, she would berate him to his wife, telling her how he was such a poor husband and how he could not be compared to the other men of the village. She told her daughter that she should never have married the hunter.

The wife listened to her mother's belittling, but she never found fault with her husband. All the same, though, the hunter's life became unbearable. His life was miserable because of the mother-in-law's constant attack upon his character and abilities. Finally, he decided to leave. He told his wife and she cried and begged him to stay. But his mind was made up. So he gave instructions to the wife that his nets, spears, bow and arrows, and snares should be saved for his two sons when they grew up. He kissed her goodbye and left the village.

He walked about the tundra for a long time and became lonely and angry toward life. He was tired of being a man and believed that other animals did not have the problems that he had, and so he wished to be something else. As he wandered the barren tundra he came upon a flock of ptarmigan. All around them were berries, green plants, and seds to eat. Life seemed so easy and simple to the birds; they appeared contented.

"Oh," said the man, "if I could only be a ptarmigan. Then I would be happy."

He watched the birds for a time and stayed close to them in hopes that they might take pity upon him and use their magic to make him become a ptarmigan. When the flock flew away to eat some place else, the hunter followed them. But every time he caught up with the flock they flew away again. He chased them like that all day until at sundown they landed just over a ridge.

When the hunter reached the place where they had landed, he found a small village of ptarmigan people. He walked into the town and straight into the kazhgie, the house where the single men lived. Inside the kazhgie were many men and boys sitting on the dirt floor.

The chief spoke to him saying, "Hunter, why have you been following my people all day upon the tundra?"

The man answered the chief, "I have followed you because I do not wish to be a man any longer. I wish to be a ptarmigan like you so that my life will be more simple."

The leader rose from his seat and stood before the man and said, "Our lives are not as pleasant as you believe. Although we have plenty of food and stay warm in our houses, many birds in the sky and beasts on the ground hunt us to eat us. Our lives are always in danger. Surely you do not wish to be like us."

The hunter had not thought of these problems before. He was tired from walking all day and so the ptarmigan people allowed him to sleep in the kazhgie. He was so tired that he fell asleep almost immediately.

When he awoke the next morning the man looked around him and saw that the entire village was gone. It had disappeared!

He collected his few belongings and continued his aimless journey upon the arctic tundra. He had not traveled long when he came upon two snow shoe rabbits playing in the brush. He watched them chasing one another and laughing as they played.

"I believe I should be very happy if I were a rabbit," said the man to himself. "I will follow them and perhaps they will take pity on me and turn me into a rabbit."

For the rest of the day the man chased the rabbits hoping to speak with them. But every time he came close enough to talk, the two rabbits ran away as fast as they could. Just at sundown the two rabbits disappeared over a hill and the man ran after them as he had done the ptarmigan.

When he came over the ridge he saw an igloo sitting upon the tundra. He walked down the hill and entered the igloo. Inside were two rabbit people preparing their beds for the night. The rabbit man asked the hunter what he wanted.

"Why have you been following us all day?" he inquired.

As the hunter told the rabbit people of his problems as a human, the two gave him some dinner. When he was finished eating, he told them how he wanted to be a rabbit so that he could live carefree as they did.

When he was finished speaking the rabbit man spoke to him again, "You would not like to be a rabbit. Large birds of prey hunt us from the air and we do not see them until it is too late. Foxes and wolves hunt us on the ground and even smaller animals sometimes eat our children. Surely you do not wish to be a helpless rabbit!"

The hunter listened and soon agreed that a rabbit's life was not as carefree a he thought. The rabbit couple invited him to stay and sleep in their igloo for the night as their guest. When he awoke in the morning, the igloo and the couple had disappeared just as the ptarmigan people had.

Once more the hunter started his quest for a better life in which no mother-in-laws berated him constantly, and in which life would be simpler.

He walked along the coastline and looked out across the sea when suddenly he saw several large bearded seals, known to the Eskimo as oogrook, swimming freely upon the surface. The hunter stopped and watched them and saw how gracefully they swam in the water. He knew that there was plenty of fish for them to eat. He thought that their life might be easy and simple and so he approached them. But every time he came close enough to speak to the seals, they quickly dived into the cold water. Finally, though, he was close enough that he could address the oogrrok and they listened.

"Please, Brother Seal," he said to the largest of the three, "I have come a long way and I wish to become one of you."

The seal swam to the edge of the ice and pulled himself up beside the Eskimo and listened as the man told him the same story he had told the ptarmigan and rabbit people. When the tale was told, he thought for a momment and then spoke to the man.

"You would not like being a seal," said the oogrook. "Although our life seems fun and simple, we are very afraid much of the time. You see, whenever we come up to our air holes in the ice, we never know if a man or polar bear is waiting to kill us."

The man had not thought of that and decided that he no longer wished to be an oogrook. Because it was very late, the seals invited him to sleep in their igloo for the night. They cooked him fish for dinner and then the man fell asleep. When he awoke in the morning the igloo and the oogrook were gone! He turned and walked back towards the tundra in search of another animal to become.

Soon the Eskimo came upon a herd of caribou grazing upon the tundra. He hid behind a thick bush and watched the herd for some time, noting how healthy and fat they were. There were so many of them that he was certain that they must be safe. From what he could see, there was no reason why he should not want to be a caribou in the herd.

So the man started towards the herd in hopes that they might use their magic to turn him into a caribou so that he could join them. However, just as the ptarmigan and rabbit people had ran when he approached them, so too did the caribou now. As before, he chased the group for the whole day and when they finally disappeared over a hill near sunset, he followed.

When he looked over the top of the hill into the valley below he saw a village with many igloos and a large kazhgie in the center. He quickly walked down to the village and entered the kazhgie. Inside were many men of all ages.

The leader of the caribou people approached him and asked, "Hunter, why have you followed us all day?"

The hunter replied, "I have watched you and wish to become one of you."

As the man related the story of his miserable life as a human, the caribou people offered him food for dinner. The Eskimo told them how he wanted to become a caribou because they seemed so safe and fat and healthy. They took pity on him and decided to make him a caribou. They promised that he would be a caribou and then invited him to spend the night in the kazhgie.

When he awoke the next morning, the village and all the igloos had disappeared. Where it had been now stood the herd of caribou grazing on the grass. He looked at himself and saw that he was a caribou, too!

For many years the hunter lived among the caribou people. He grew to be fat, strong, and fleet-footed. Although wolves chased the herd and killed many brothers throughout the years, he always escaped. Hunters from villages sometimes hunted the herd, but he

managed to escape their traps and spears as well. He was content with his new life.

But after many years the man began to wonder about his wife. He wondered if she had remarried, and whether the mother-in-law was still alive. He especially wondered about his two sons. So one day he approached the leader of the caribou people and said that he wanted to return to his life as a man.

The leader sympathized with the hunter and gave him instructions to follow, but he warned that it would be difficult to become a man again after being a caribou for so long.

The hunter thanked the chief and left for his village, still a caribou. It took him many days and he had to avoid traps and snares, and even hunters themselves, but he finally reached his village upon the sea.

As he walked towards his old house he stepped into a snare and was trapped. Shortly, two young men came out and were surprised to have caught a caribou so close to their house. When they approached to kill him, the caribou man spoke in a human voice.

"Please release me and skin the fur from my head," he said.

The two men were shocked. They had never heard a caribou speak before. But the caribou repeated his request again and the young men finally agreed and skinned the fur from his head. When they finished, they saw that it was a man inside the skin. The caribou man asked them to continue until he was completely a man again.

When they had finished they took the man to their home. When he entered their house he was surprised, for there was his wife and she recognized her long-lost husband. She told him that she had never remarried because she had waited for him, knowing that he would return one day. The two young men who had snared him were his own two sons now grown to manhood. The old mother-in-law had died many years before.

The old hunter was at last happy to be a man. He lived with his wife and they were very happy until they died of old age.

Stone Woman

Upon the flat arctic tundra, the horizon never seems to change and there is nothing to compare distances. About a decade ago, I walked much of the Arctic Ocean and Chukchi Sea coastline while collecting data for the U. S. Geological Survey Department. In several places I came upon stone erections in human form. There are reasons for these "statues" and numerous legends about their origin. The following tale was told to me by a native colleague at Alaska Pacific University while I was a graduate student there.

It is said that a group of hunters, young and old men alike, once left their small village to hunt whales and ugruk in their kayaks and umiaks. Like most hunting trips, the men planned to be away for many days while in search of game.

One of the young men on the hunt had just taken one of the lovely young women of the village for his wife. But when the other men left in their boats, he joined them so that he could provide meat for his wife and himself.

Although the newly-wed wife would miss him, she knew that he was a good hunter and that he would soon return with enough food for the winter. She kissed him goodbye and busied herself while he was gone.

The very next day a terrible storm tormented the sea, creating high and dangerous waves. It lasted for many days and all of the villagers worried about the hunters. The older men, who were now too old to hunt with the others, said that they had never before seen the sea so terrible. Everyone watched for the hunters.

After a long time, one of the two umiaks arrived. All the men were in it except the young woman's husband. The chief told the villagers how the other boats had been destroyed and how the one man had fallen into the water. Although they had searched for him, the hunters had not found his body.

The newly-wed woman would not accept her husband's death and so she went up to the hill overlooking the sea and sat upon a rock to watch and wait for his return. Her family brought her food and water and after weeks tried to convince her to come home. But she told them that she would wait until he returned.

One day, after several months, the woman's younger sister went up the hill to bring her food and found that she had turned into a statue of stone which still looks out over the sea in the direction where her beloved husband had been lost.

A Story Of Raven

There are numerous Alaskan native legends of Raven
tricking, and sometimes killing other animals with his
deceit. But this Eskimo tale is one of the few where he
tricks, kills, and eats humans.

It is said that a very long time ago Raven used to eat people
because they were so easy to trick.

One day, while flying high over the arctic coastline, Raven
saw a small village. He was very hungry so he made a plan to get
food to eat. He flew low over the village screaming, "Your
enemies are coming! Your enemies are coming!"

All of the men ran out of their igloos with their spears in
hand and asked the great bird what they should do.

Raven landed on top of a cache and addressed the men, "You
must surprise them before they reach your village. Go and make
camp at the foot of the cliff and wait for them in the morning."

The unsuspecting men thanked Raven and set out for the cliff's
base to ambush the attackers in the morning as he had said to do.

When they arrived that night they built shelters at the foot
of the steep cliff where Raven had told them to do so. Later that
night, after the men had discussed their plans and strategies,
their seal oil lamps were extinguished and they all went to
sleep.

Once it was dark and the men were asleep, Raven flew to the
top of the cliff high above the small camp and landed on an
enormous overhang of heavy snow. Raven knew that the great load
of snow was ready to fall with only the slightest encouragement,
and so he proceeded to jump up and down upon it.

After a few jumps, the overhang collapsed and avalanched down
upon the sleeping men. They were completely buried alive by the
heavy snow load!

The snow was very deep and because Raven was lazy and didn't
want to work to dig the dead men out so that he could eat them,
he waited until spring when the snow melted, then he returned to
eat them all.

The sun had melted the snow to expose the bodies of the
unfortunate people. Raven was very pleased that he would have so
much meat to eat. He liked to peck out the eyes of his victims
and then eat the eyeballs. For the entire spring he stayed there
at the bottom of the cliff gorging himself on the warriors who
had listened to his trickery and deceit.

How Light Was Brought Into The World

Almost every Alaskan native group has a myth which explains the origin of light in the world. Whereas in the Tlingit legend Raven steals the sun, moon, and stars, in this Eskimo tale it is a man who undertakes a journey and steals the sun.

In the beginning, there was only night. It was very dark and there was no light except that which came from campires and seal oil lamps. Hunters had to hunt in darkness and the caribou had to stumble in the blackness in search of food.

One day, a brave young man decided to travel the world in search of light. When spring came he crafted the strongest and fastest kayak ever made, and filled it with dried fish and seal bladders full of fresh water. When this was all done, he pushed his kayak into the sea and paddled away from his village in search of Day. His mother cried because she was certain that she would never see him again, but the villagers waved good-bye as he disappeared in the horizon because they hoped that he would find light and bring Day into the world.

The man paddled for many days. When he became hungry he stopped to eat. When he was thirsty he drank from the bladder bags; and when he became tired, he slept. Since there was no such thing then as day to contrast night, people slept only when they grew tired.

Whenever a whale swam near him, the man asked if it knew where he would find Day. But none of the creatures of the sea knew about light.

After a very long time on the water, the man came upon an island. He pulled his boat up onto the land, ate some dried fish and whale fat, and then went to sleep. When he awoke the next morning he saw a very strange thing. A bright round ball was coming up from the edge of the ocean. As it did, it lit the sky around it and the man could even feel warmth coming from the glowing ball.

He watched it for several hours, wondering where it came from. Finally, it began to go down at the place where it came up. Once it sank into the water Night came again and it became dark.

The man decided to camp at the island and to wait until the ball appeared. Then, he decided, he would paddle in the direction until he found the sun.

The next day, when the brilliant ball came up again, the man immediately launched his kayak and paddled in the direction as fast as he could.

When he finally reached the land where the light came from, the ball had already gone down and it was dark again. The man set out on foot to find the sun. In the distance he saw a large house and a bright light was shining from within it.

Quietly, he crept up to the small opening and looked inside the room. There was a person sleeping on the dirt floor and beside him was the large, bright ball. It was so bright that the man could not look at it because it hurt his eyes.

He looked away into the darkness outside and thought, "This man must let the ball out of the house sometimes. When he does, it is daytime. When he brings it back inside, it is night."

The brave young man watched for a long time. When he was certain that the guardian was asleep, he looked into the window again and then he snuck into the room towards the bright ball. He finally managed to get close enough to grab the thing called Day. Once he had it safely outside, he started to run to his kayak, still carrying the sun.

Just before he reached the boat, he heard an angry voice behind him yelling, "Stop! Give me back my light. Give me back the sun!"

But the man only ran faster and then threw the bright ball into his boat and jumped in himself. The other man did not have a kayak and so he escaped with Day.

When he finally reached his own village, the man released Day into the world. Since that time there has always been day and night so that Eskimo know when to sleep and when to hunt.

The Greedy Husband

This Eskimo tale is very much like the didactic Western
story of the lazy grasshopper who doesn't prepare for
winter, and the hard-working ants who do. It moralizes
through an opposite illustration the Eskimo concept of
how husband and wife relationships should be.

Once there was an Eskimo man and woman who were married as
husband and wife. They lived in a small village where a river
emptied into the ocean. They had not been married very long when
one day the man went seal hunting.

After several days he returned home dragging a large seal. She
was very happy that her young husband had killed a seal because
now they would have plenty of food and seal oil for their light
and cooking stove.

The woman ran out of their home to meet him and to help him
drag it to the house. He refused to let her help him, and when
she offered to help cut it up he refused her again.

"I will do it myself!" was his stearn reply.

She asked if she could cook some of the meat for their supper.

"No," he answered, "I shall cook it and eat it myself."

So the man prepared the seal and ate it himself. He didn't
give his young wife any of it. The woman was very hurt, she had
never seen her husband behave in such a way, and because he would
not feed her, she moved away from their home to live by herself
in another part of the village.

Because she could not hunt well by herself, the woman gathered
berries and dried fish to eat. Sometimes people in the village
would trade her oil and seal skin for her berries; and so she was
not starving.

When the long winter came, there was a famine in the village
and everyone was hungry except the woman because she had gathered
and saved plenty of food for the winter.

One day her greedy husband came to her small house to ask for
food because he had none. You see, he had not stored any meat or
oil for the winter.

"I want some of your berries and dried salmon," he said.

He was not asking for the food, instead, he was telling her to
give them to him even though it was she who worked to gather it.

The woman remembered how her husband had not shared any of his
seal with her and how he would have her starve to death. He did
not give her one mouthful of food.

"No," she said. "I am going to feed myself."

This was the same thing he had told her earlier when she asked to help prepare and cook the seal.

The man was thin from not eating for weeks. He just looked at her and repeated his demand.

"Give me some of your berries and dried fish."

The woman again replied that she would not and as she did, she began to prepare herself a bowl of Eskimo ice cream, which is berries mixed with seal oil.

The man was too weak to argue or force her to give up the food, and so he just watched as she ate all of the ice cream herself. When she was finished, she threw one single berry onto the floor and told him that he could have it.

In the darkly lit house he searched the dirt floor for the berry. But he was so weak from starvation, that he collapsed and died before he found the small morsel.

Kajortoq, The White Fox

Raven is not the only animal to play mean and sometimes deadly tricks on other animals. In this story, Kajortoq, a hungry and witty white fox, outsmarts two animals to satisfy her hunger. In the end, though, it is Raven who outwits Kajortoq.

A very long time ago when the animals could talk, Kajortoq, the white fox, was walking along the tundra in the springtime when she saw a caribou grazing on moss. Kajortoq was very hungry and so she thought of a plan so that she could eat the caribou.

Cautiously she approached the large animal and said to it, "I know of a place where there is a big patch of tasty moss."

The caribou, who had previously ignored the small white fox, now looked up with interest and listened.

"Yes," continued the devious Kajortoq, "I saw a place only this morning with so much fresh and delicious moss that it would take days for you to eat it all."

The caribou wondered where such a place was and so asked the white fox.

"It is on a trail which runs along the edge of the cliff which overlooks the sea," she replied.

The caribou thought to itself, "This little white fox surely cannot harm me."

And so he agreed to follow Kajortoq to the food.

The small fox led the caribou to the trail which ran along a steep cliff down towards the beach below. It was a very narrow path and the small rocks on it were very loose and wet, making the going dangerously rough and slippery. Far below, the caribou could see the waves crashing upon the large, jagged rocks on the beach.

Noticing his slight hesitation, Kajortoq enticed the caribou by reminding him of the reward at the other end of the trail.

"There is so much delicious, fresh moss and lichens that it will take you days to eat it all," she reiterated.

They began to move down the precarious path. The caribou was not as graceful as the small white fox, and several times he stumbled on some loose rock and almost fell.

Frequently, Kajortoq turned around and warned her unsuspecting prey as if she were truly a good friend.

"Be careful here. You wouldn't want to fall. Don't lose your footing," and so on.

Finally, though, they came to a place where the trail had been all but destroyed by a landslide. The trail continued on the far side where the landslide had been, but it was quite a jump to reach it.

"We must jump. The food is just on the other side," she said.

But the caribou was scared and would not move.

"It is not so difficult. I easily jumped across it only this morning," lied the small, hungry white fox. "Jump quickly and do not think about it!"

The caribou did as the fox demanded and jumped. When it landed on the other side of the trail, its hooves slipped on the loose rocks which were wet from the morning dew, and he fell to the jagged rocks far below.

Kajortoq laughed as she slowly descended the narrow trail to the beach below where the dead caribou lay. She danced around the body and sang a song about how she had tricked the caribou and how she now would have plenty of meat to eat.

The meal lasted for many days, but finally everything was eaten and so she left to find someone else to trick for food.

Out on the tundra again, she came across a ptarmigan sitting on her eggs in a nest in the branches of a tall shrub.

She looked up at he mother ptarmigan and said, "Give me one of your eggs to eat."

The bird was afraid for all of her eggs and so she agreed to give up one if she promised to go away afterwards.

Kajortoq agreed and so the mother ptarmigan let one egg fall to the ground where the fox greedily devoured it and then left.

The very next day, however, the white fox returned demanding another egg.

"No!" said the mother. "I gave you one yesterday and you promised to leave the others alone."

Kajortoq grew angry and yelled up at Ptarmigan, "Give me another egg or I will use my axe to cut down the tree. Then I will eat all of your eggs and perhaps even you if I catch you."

Again, the mother bird was frightened and so she let fall another one of her eggs which the selfish fox quickly ate and then left as she had done the first time.

Raven had been flying high above both times and came down to speak with Ptarmigan.

"Friend Ptarmigan," he said, "Kajortoq has tricked you. She does not have an axe to cut down your tree. You and your eggs are safe. Do not let her take any more eggs from you."

The mother bird thanked the wise Raven and waited for the fox to return.

The very next day Kajortoq returned demanding another egg.

When she refused, the white fox again threatened to cut down the tree with an axe.

"I am safe here, Fox. You cannot get me or my eggs," replied the brave ptarmigan.

Kajortoq was furious and asked, "Who has told you lies about me?"

Ptarmigan replied, "Brother Raven has spoken with me and told me that you do not have an axe and that I am safe from you."

Now angry and hungry, the small white fox walked away and made a plan to get even with Raven.

She purposely limped out into a large open area acting as if she were wounded. Then she lay down and quietly waited for Raven to come.

Raven watched from high overhead and after a time flew down and landed near the seemingly dead fox. Cautiously, he approached and then pecked at the fox's hind legs to see if she was indeed dead. Kajortoq remained still, fooling Raven into believing that she was dead.

When the great black bird walked around to the front of the fox to peck out her eyes so that he could eat them, Kajortoq quickly pounced on the bird and grabbed him in her strong jaws.

Still alive, she carried him towards her den.

Raven was worried and mad that he had been so cleverly tricked and so he made a plan to escape.

After some careful thought he asked the fox, "Why does it snow in the winter?"

The white fox thought about the question and then responded in amazement, "That is a crazy question. Why did you ask that?"

But just as soon as she opened her mouth to speak, Raven jumped out and flew away, laughing at the fox as he did so.

In anger, Kajortoq walked off muttering to herself while looking for someone else to trick.

Athabaskan

Skolce's, A Rabbit Tale

I first heard this Ahtna legend many years ago while visiting in the Copper Center region where my family originates. This strangely humorous tale depicts how rabbits, which once had dangerously sharp tails, got to have soft, bent, "powder puff" tails.

A long time ago, an Ahtna Indian from Tazlina went hunting along the river nearby where it empties into the mighty Copper River. He hunted all day and when it became dark he made camp along the river bank. He lay down to rest and the sound of the running water quickly put him to sleep.

After he was gone for several days, some of the other men from his village went to search for him. They followed the trail along the Tazlina River until they came to the Copper River. There, they found the dead hunter with a small, round hole cut in his throat. They took his body back to his family and thought little of the mysterious death.

After a while, though, another man went hunting in the same place and when he didn't return, the village men searched for him and found him dead with the same small puncture in the throat.

The people began to become scared. They did not know what was happening to the hunters, but they were sure that they did not want to die in the same way. The men were so frightened that they stopped hunting except in broad daylight and even then, only near the village. The food supplies began to run low. The dried salmon was almost gone and the people were getting hungry.

The problem became worse and worse until one Ahtna man, Ciil Hwyaa, decided to find out what was happening. He left early one morning and followed the very same trail the other two men had walked. He hunted along the way and when he came to the place where the Tazlina flows into the Copper, he built a small camp.

Ciil Hwyaa had seen nothing strange on his journey, but he knew that this was the same place where the other two men had died. Because he was a very smart man, he collected several large flat rocks from along the river's edge and placed them under his clothes; one under his clothes where his heart is, and the other he placed upon his throat. He covered it so that it could not be seen. Once he had done these things, he pretended to go to sleep. He closed his eyes but he was not really asleep. He was waiting for something to come and kill him.

Very late that night, when he was almost asleep, Ciil Hwyaa heard a thumping noise coming up the trail and he opened his eyes

105

just a little and saw that it was only a rabbit. The small rabbit walked up to him and then jumped up in the air and landed on the man's neck with his sharp tail pointed downward.

You   see, rabbits had sharp, pointed tails in the days of long ago which were used to protect themselves from other animals. But this little, mischievous rabbit had been using it to kill Indians while they were asleep!

When the rabbit jumped on Ciil Hwyaa's throat, his tail landed right on the flat rock which made his sharp, pointed tail become bent! The rabbit started screaming in pain and ran away into the forest.

The   hunter   returned to his village and told the people what had happened. No one was ever killed by rabbits again and from that time on all rabbits have bent tails.

Lake Monster

When I was a child driving along the Glenn Highway, my grandmother, an Ahtna Indian whose father was Tazlina Joe of the Talcheena Clan, told me the story of a giant and ferocious monster that lives in Tazlina and Klutina Lakes, both of which are glacial-fed and quite large. This is the Ahtna version of the Loch Ness monster in Scotland.

Before there was ever white men in Ahtna territory, the hunters used to hunt and fish on Tazlina Lake and Klutina Lake. Klutina is a big lake, almost nineteen miles long. Tazlina is a large, somewhat circular lake. You can see it from the road to Lake Louise and along the Glenn highway near Mendelta. Both are deep and are fed by melting glaciers at their headwater.

In the old days, Indians would walk to Tazlina Lake by following the Tazlina River near Copper Center. Nowadays their is a seven mile trail near Mendelta. Klutina Lake trail begins near Tazlina and is more than twenty miles long. Both lakes are full of fish, and big game is abundant in the region. The Nelchina caribou herd migrates through the Tazlina Lake area in great numbers. My grandmother's sister, Morrie Secondchief, once told me that the herd migrated into Canada in the early part of this century and did not return to Ahtna territory until about 1925.

Once in a while, in the old days, hunters would see a strange creature swimming in the lakes. There are very few descriptions of the monster, but all accounts agree that it was quite large. Sometimes, a herd of caribou would be seen swimming across the middle of one of the lakes and all of a sudden a large caribou would be quickly and violently pulled beneath the water.

Because of their fear that a monster might kill them, Ahtna men avoided the middle of the lakes where it was very deep and rough.

Stone Woman

Along the Glenn Highway, somewhere between King Mountain and Sheep Mountain, just north east of the Matanuska Glacier, there is a giant stone mountain perhaps a thousand feet tall. Ahtna Indians call it "Stone Woman Mountain" and they have a legend about its creation. The tale is slightly reminiscent of the biblical account of Lot's wife.

In Ahtna, the Talcheena Clan literally means "People from the Sea". It is believed that long ago the people moved into the Interior where they would find better hunting and fishing grounds. This story is about what happened to one woman while making the long journey into traditional Ahtna territory.

Back then, a long time ago, people were giants. They were very big and a hungry man could eat an entire whale at one sitting. It is thought that they lived near Cook Inlet and Prince William Sound, but one day they decided to move into the Interior so they began the long trek.

Between them and their new villages of Tazlina, Gukona, Gulkana, Mentasta, Chitna, Copper Center, Mendelta, Chickaloon, Chistochina, Cantwell, and Tonsina was a great mountain range that was so high that many glaciers and rivers are born there and the snow never melts in the summertime.

Raven decided to help them and he used his power to make it so that they could easily climb the rugged mountains and get to their new land. But he told them that once they made it over the great mountains, that they must not look back to see where they had come from. If they did, Raven told them, something terrible would happen.

The people marched for many days and when they finally crossed the range into Ahtna territory, one woman who was carrying her baby on her back, turned to look back because she missed her old home already. No sooner did she look back than she turned to stone! She became a giant stone statue! Raven had warned them not to look back, but she didn't listen to him and so something terrible happened to her.

Today, you can still see her standing in the valley with her baby on her back.

Raven Steals The Light

A similar account of this oral narrative appears in Eskimo mythology. The Tanaina legend below from Nondalton closely resembles another Athabaskan tale by the Upper Tanana Indians of Tetlin and Northway. In that version, however, Raven becomes a piece of moss.

There once lived a very powerful and rich chief who had a beautiful young daughter. Somehow, the chief got the sun and the moon and he hung them up in his house. Because he had the sun and the moon, it became dark everywhere.

Because of the darkness, the people could not hunt or fish. When they went out to find wood to burn in their fires, they had to crawl around in the forest feeling with their hands until they found something which might be wood. Then they would bite it to make certain that it was indeed firewood.

Raven learned that the great chief had taken the sun and moon, so he went to his house to take it back. He asked the chief if he would return the sun and moon, but he would not. So the smart black bird devised a plan.

He saw how the chief's daughter went to a small stream to get water every morning, so he hid near there and waited for her to return. When he saw her coming down the trail, he turned himself into a fingerling, a tiny fish, and jumped into the water. After the girl arrived, she filled a bucket with water. Then she dipped her drinking cup into the stream and Raven, disguised as a fingerling, quickly swam into it. She did not see Raven and drank the water.

Inside her body, Raven turned into a baby and so the girl became pregnant. After a short time the daughter gave birth to a baby boy which was really Raven. The baby grew fast and was soon a young boy. The grandfather was very fond of his grandson and would do anything for him. One day the boy began crying for something.

The chief asked him, "What do you want, grandson?"

The boy pointed to the sun and moon hanging from the ceiling. The chief decided to let him play with them if it would make him stop crying. So the boy took them outside and played with them for a while, but then he threw them high into the air. When the old chief ran out to see what had happened, Raven became himself again and flew away. Since that time there has been light.

The Loon Story

This story, like that of Raven stealing the sun, moon, and stars, is represented in most every Alaskan Native oral tradition and appears in Inupiaq, Yupik, Eyak, Ahtna, and Upper Tanana ethnography. The following is an account from the Upper Tanana Indians.

In a small village beyond Northway just south of the upper Tanana River, there once was a man who lived with his wife and young son. There were many lakes and wet bogs behind the small village where the people hunted moose and ducks, and even caught many fish there.

The man was a great hunter and each time he went hunting, he always returned with a moose or something to eat. It is said that he was so accurate with his bow that he could hit a low flying duck or goose with one shot.

A few years after his marriage, though, his eye-sight began to become poor. He could still see a little light on a sunny day, but he could not clearly see objects any longer so his wife had to lead him everywhere.

Because he could no longer see well, the man could not hunt and so the family began to run out of food. Their relatives in the village wuld give them some of their food, but times were tough and so they could not spare much meat.

Because the once great hunter was now handicapped, the wife became cruel to him. When she received fish and meat from the villagers, she would not give much of it to him. The people were giving her food because of her poor blind husband, and yet she didn't share with him and even lied about the food she got telling him that there was none. Because he was blind, she thought that he wouldn't find out. This went on for a long time and the blind man was starving.

One day they went hunting for small rabbits and grouse. While they were setting up camp the man heard something nearby.

"Listen," he said. "I hear a moose feeding."

They stopped to listen and soon they too heard the moose nearby.

"Get my bow and guide me to the moose," he instructed his wife and young son. "I know that I can kill it if I am close enough."

So the mean woman took her blind husband by the arm and led him close to the large moose. He listened for a moment and then raised his powerful bow and let loose an arrow. The arrow flew straight and hit the moose in the heart. It died instantly.

Even though he had killed the moose, the woman lied to him and said that he had missed. She acted angry and insulted him saying how poor a hunter he was and how worthless he was to his family.

But the man had heard the sound of his arrow striking the moose and was certain that he had hit it, but the wicked woman convinced him that he was wrong.

The wife led the man to a stump and told him that she was going to take their young son to look for grouse and rabbits. She left him there and after not returning for a long time, the man thought that she had left him to die. Actually, she went to skin the moose. She built a drying rack between the trees and cut up the meat. She was going to eat it all and never tell the husband about it.

The man sat there throughout the night and he was very cold. The next day he crawled along the trail using his hands to feel the way. After a while he came upon a small lake where he heard a loon. The man drank from the lake and felt somewhat refreshed. Just then the loon swam close to him and spoke in his language.

"What is wrong with you?" it asked.

The man had never heard a loon speak before, but answered him anyhow.

"I can no longer see. I have become blind and cannot hunt or find my way home," he said.

The loon said that he could help and instructed him to climb onto his great back. The man felt his way to the bird and did as he said. When he was on, the bird dove beneath the surface. When he came up, he told the man to open his eyes and asked if he could see.

"I can barely make out the shoreline," he replied.

So the loon dove twice more and this time the man could see very well, even better than before he became blind. He thanked the loon and promised never to hunt his people in the future and then left for home.

When the man walked into their home the woman was surprised and angry. She wanted him to die out in the woods so that she could get a new husband. He pretended that he was still blind and when she asked how he made it home, he told her that he felt his way to the village.

Then he said that he was thristy and asked for a drink of water. The mean wife brought him a cup of greenish water which was full of bugs and insect larvae. You see, she had been giving him this water ever since he was blind.

At dinner time, the woman, still thinking her husband was blind, cooked herself some moose ribs and gave the husband the bones when she was finished eating. Then she went out to get some more meat from the drying rack and the husband followed her.

She heard something coming and turned around. There was the husband standing just behind her. He told her that he could see now because the loon had used his magic to help him. The hunter asked his son if he wanted to live with him and he agreed to. So they moved away to the other side of the village.

The people of the village wondered how he could see again but agreed that he did the right thing by leaving his selfish and cruel wife.

From then on, the man was a great hunter, even better than before, and he always shared his meat with the poor, sick, blind, and aged.

The Old Man And The Bear

This Tanacross Indian tale, from the area around Tok and Tanacross, depicts the pride and respect the elderly deserve. In all my studies, I have found very little documented folklore from this region.

Back before white men were searching for gold in Alaska, there was a village near where Tanacross is today. It was mid-summer and the salmon were running strong in the Tanana, so there was plenty of fish drying for the winter months.

Some young boys wanted to go look for moose and an old man asked if he could go with them. So they all went walking along the trail to Bailey Lake looking for moose.

When they got close, they saw a large grizzly bear on the hill side just below them. The boys started to yell at it. They were teasing it, but it ignored them and kept walking in the same direction.

The boys were angry that it was ignoring them and so they teased it more saying that it was afraid of a bunch of young boys. The old man told them to stop, saying that it was not wise to bother the big bear, but they kept on yelling anyhow.

The grizzly stopped and looked up at the boys. Then it started walking up the hill towards them. The boys were scared and they all ran away, leaving the old man alone to face the angry bear.

When it got close, the big bear charged the old man. All the man had was a walking stick, so he jumped up and yelled at the bear. The bear didn't know what to think and so he just stopped right there and sat back.

The old man wasted no time. He hit the bear across the nose, knocking it over. Then he hit it over the head until it was dead. The old man had killed a grizzly bear with only a walking stick!

He started to skin the animal and after a while the boys came back and saw what he had done. From then on those boys respected what the old man told them and never teased bears again.

A Mouse Story

This brief tale was originally told in Deg Hit'an Athabaskan and later translated into Upper Kuskokwim Athabaskan. Unlike most legends and myths, it doesn't particularly teach any message or account for the origin of things.

Tildzidza, the mouse, lived in a small underground house along the banks of the Kuskokwim River. One day he was walking upstream following the beach looking for something to do.

He was bored and wanted something to do. He took out one of his front teeth and started to play with it. He threw it up in the air and caught it. He rolled it across his hand playing with it. He ran along the beach playing with his tooth, when all of a sudden he tripped and dropped it.

He looked for the tooth, but it was lost. He searched for a long time in the tall grass, but he never found it. Tildzidza was mad because he had lost his front tooth, so he took off up river again. He was very angry but he wanted something else to do now.

After walking a short distance, the mouse came upon a little hill from which a plume of smoke was rising like a tiny volcano. He walked to it so that he could see it better. There were berries growing all around the little mound, all kinds of berries. Tildzidza began to eat them. He ate all of the berries he could find until he was full.

When he was finished eating, he went back to his little house to rest. That is all.

Beaver And Fox

This brief Alaskan Native tale comes from the Han Indians, whose traditional liguistic territory ranges along the Yukon River and into Canada. In 1982 there were only 20 Alaskan Han Indians who still spoke the language. This particular story was told by a native living at Eagle, only a few miles from the Canadian border.

Although Beaver was usually busy building dams, he decided to go visit his friend, the fox. Beaver's house was just upstream of the mouth where a small creek emptied into a lake. Fox's den was along the banks overlooking the lake where he could spot small rabbits and birds near the water. Because they lived fairly close to each other, they were good friends.

When Beaver found his friend he said, "Let's take a walk together along the trail."

Fox thought it was a good idea, so they walked down the trail together. But Fox kept making Beaver mad all the time because he was so fast and he was jumping and frolicking all the time.

You see, Beaver's tail was wet from swimming and it was heavy. This made him walk slowly and he could not keep up with his friend.

"You're tail is too heavy," said Fox to his friend.

Beaver was becoming mad with Fox and told him so.

"Why are you always making fun of my tail?" he asked. "You're the one with the silly tail. Why, your tail is useless. At least mine helps me swim. What good is yours?"

Then they both started laughing because they were arguing over their tails. They agreed that both of their tails were funny and so they walked on together laughing.

After a while, they went back home.

The Rich Chief's Son

This tale from the Tanaina Athabaskans, also spelled Dena'ina, is sometimes called "The Mouse Story". Like the "Ptarmigan" story told in Yupik Eskimo, this tale illustrates how natives must respect the animals and what the consequences of breaking the taboo might be.

Long ago, in the village of Nondalton, or was it Tyonek, there lived a very rich man who had a lazy son. This young man was very lazy. He never worked and always made everyone else do his chores. Because his father was a powerful chief, he even had several slaves which he had captured from other villages. The son made these slaves do all his work for him.

One day, the lazy son's mother was cooking fish soup and asked him to watch the boiling pot and scoop out the fatty grease which floated to the top when the salmon was cooking. Of course the lazy son complained that it was too much work, but the mother made him do it and so he tried.

He stood near the kettle but paid little attention to it. Once in a while he carelessly scooped out a bit of the grease.

While he was standing there he noticed a small mouse running around the floor. He watched it and when it came close enough he scooped some scalding hot grease from the boiling soup and threw it upon the poor little mouse. The mouse's back was scorched and scalded and it almost died, but it somehow made it back to its hole. The lazy and cruel young man thought nothing of what he had done and went about carelessly watching the salmon soup. He didn't tell anyone about what he had done.

Shortly after the incident winter came. The leaves fell from the trees and snow covered the ground. The people had dried plenty of meat and fish for the long, cold winter. But they were not prepared for this particular winter. It was always cold and there was no game to be found anywhere. Even the ice-fishing holes produced nothing. Soon, the food ran out and the people began to starve.

The elders of the village said that there had never been so severe a winter and they wondered if someone had broken a taboo. The lazy son began to think about what he had done and decided that it was all his fault. He dressed in his warmest parka and, taking his bow and arrows, left the village in seacrh of the answer.

In the woods, he came upon a mouse den. He listened carefully and heard a tiny woman's voice telling him to close his eyes and

118

turn around three times while covering his eyes with his sleeve. Then he was told to place his head against the ground.

The lazy young man did as he was told and suddenly he fell into the house. He had shrunk so that he was now standing in the mouse's house! He saw a young woman sitting there. She motioned him to come close to her and then she spoke to him.

"There is a terrible famine in your village," she said.

"I wanted you to come here and that is why you are here now, because I willed it," she continued.

The man just stood there looking around in disbelief.

Then the mouse-woman spoke again.

"Do you remember what you did this summer?" she asked. "Do you recall doing something wrong?"

The rich man's son recalled how he had poured scalding hot salmon soup grease on the poor little mouse.

"Yes!" answered the young man.

"That was my child you hurt," she said and she walked over to a curtain and pulled it back. Behind it was a young child lying on a small bed. His body was badly scalded and swollen and he was in terrible pain.

"This is why there is a famine in your village," said the mother mouse.

The lazy man looked at the poor mouse-child and was saddened.

"I am very sorry," he said. "I did not know what I had done. I did not mean to hurt him."

There was nothing to do for the child, so the mother told the man never to harm small animals again. Then she told him to cover his eyes as before and turn three times. He did this and soon he was back outside the small mouse den.

On his way home, the rich man's son came across ten caribou and he shot every one of them with his bow. He cut them up and packed one of them back to his village. The people were starving and were too weak to move, so the young man walked back to the caribou and carried each one to the village. It took him ten trips to get all the meat to the villagers and he did all of the work alone! He was no longer lazy. He became a good hunter and a hard worker.

How Raven Killed The Whale

Although only the Tanaina (Dena'ina) Athabaskan's traditional territory borders the ocean, surrounding much of Cook Inlet, this legend is found in Upper Tanana and Koyukon Athabaskan folklore as well. That whales don't exist in the Interior suggests that either the people of Alaska originally lived along the sea, or that exchange of information is predominate among the various indigenous populations.

As usual, Raven was hungry. He had heard of a large whale near an island and so he went to see it for himself. The people in the village near the whale were afraid of it, and they were too scared to go fishing.

Raven flew to the place and watched the whale for three days hoping to think of a way to trick it. You see, The smart bird knew that he would have lots of meat if he could kill the whale.

Finally, an idea came to him and he walked up close to the whale who was resting near shore.

"Please come closer, Cousin Whale, so that I may speak with you," requested Raven.

Whale opened his eyes and slowly swam up to the small black bird and asked what he wanted.

"I have come to tell you that we are cousins," responded the trickster.

"That is impossible! You are a bird and I am a whale. We cannot be relatives," said the great whale.

"Oh," said Raven, "it is true and I can prove it to you."

The whale was curious and asked how he could prove their relation.

"If you open your mouth," said Raven, "I will show you how our throats are the same shape, which proves that we are cousins."

Although the giant whale was not completely satisfied, he was soon opening his mouth for Raven nonetheless.

When the creature's mouth was open far enough, Raven ran into his mouth and down his throat. He was wearing a backpack with his knife and some firewood in it, and once inside he cut meat from the whale and cooked it over a small fire.

Whale knew that he had been tricked so he pleaded with Raven not to eat his heart. Raven agreed at the time and spent many days living inside the whale's body eating his meat whenever he grew hungry, which was most of the time.

Once most of the flesh had been cooked and eaten, Raven began to pull out Whale's organs as well. He ate his liver and other parts, but left the heart.

One day, Whale told Raven that the water was getting shallower and that they were near land. Raven took his knife and cut out Whale's heart and ate it, killing the great creature immediately.

The dead body washed up onto shore but Raven could not get out because the giant mouth was closed. He stayed inside the whale for another few days eating the rib cage.

On the third day he heard the voices of men outside. It was a group of hunters who had found the whale carcass. As soon as the people cut the whale open, Raven flew out and escaped.

Raven and Goose-Wife

Whereas many Alaskan birds migrate annually to warmer climates, Raven always stays near his people. In this Eagle Han tale, Raven once tried to fly away with the geese, but decided to stay in Alaska forever.

It is said that Raven once fell in love with a beautiful young goose girl. They stayed together all summer long, but when fall came and snow was soon to arrive, the goose girl wanted to join her relatives to fly south. Raven decided to go with her because he loved her so much and she would not stay.

Now Raven can fly as good as any other bird, but he cannot fly very far at one time. He tried to keep up with the large flock, but he was always growing tired and had to rest often. When the geese did stop to sleep and eat, they always stopped at places where there was no food for Raven. Because of this, he was becoming weaker every day.

The geese were in a hurry to get away from the coming cold and they did not like waiting for Raven all the time. His goose-wife let him ride on her back, but because he was so heavy she couldn't carry him for long. The girl's folks carried Raven for a while, too, but they soon grew tired as well. They took turns like that until they came to the ocean.

The girl's father told Raven that the ocean was very far across and that there would be no place to land and rest. He told him that they could not make it with him on their backs.

Raven thought about this and decided that he would have to stay. He said good-bye to his beloved goose-wife, and then he flew home where he has lived since. Now ravens live here all the time because they can't fly across the ocean like the geese.

Dotson' Sa, Great Raven Makes The World

This is a wonderful narrative, told in Koyukuk and Upper Kuskokwim, in which Dotson' Sa, the Great Raven, creates the world. In it, there is a global flood such as that found in <u>Genesis</u> in the Judeo-Christian biblical account, and Raven himself acts as Noah.

A very, very long time ago, giant animals lived in the world and there was no such thing as mankind. They were all big and could talk to each other and use magic. There were even some animals which no longer live on earth.

One day Dotson' Sa, Great Raven, said to Raven, "Make a large raft."

So Raven made a large boat. It took a long time because it had to be very big. When Raven was finished, Dotson' Sa told him it wasn't big enough.

"You must build it bigger," he said.

When it was finished, it began to rain. At first it rained only a little and Dotson' Sa instructed Raven to gather all of the animals in pairs. Raven gathered the animals and food for them. It was very difficult but he did it anyhow.

Once all of the animals were on the raft, it started to rain very hard. The whole world was soon flooded and only those animals on the raft were left in the world.

When it stopped raining Raven asked some seagulls to fly in every direction in search of land. They flew away and returned saying how there was no land in sight. There was only water!

After a while the food was almost gone. Raven told Muskrat to swim down to the ocean floor to make an island. The muskrat, who was really quite large, dived down and started piling up the mud from the bottom. He kept this up until land appeared.

Dotson' Sa used his magic and made berries, trees, and plants cover the land. When he had done this, lakes and ponds were left where there had been low spots in the land. Next, Great Raven made rivers. He made them so that they flowed both ways! On one side the river ran down to the sea, and on the other it flowed up towards the mountains!

Later, though, he decided that it was too easy to travel and so he made it so that rivers only went down to the sea.

Now that the flood was gone and there was land, Dotson' Sa decided to make man. He created him from stone but because he was made of rock, man would never die and so Great Raven decided to make him from clay instead.

After he had made man, he made woman so that they could be married and have children. Raven wanted a wife so he tried to marry one of the women but the men took her away from him. This made Raven mad, so he took some dried leaves and crushed them into a large bag. He took the bag and went to where the people lived and opened it. Out flew millions of mosquitos which still pester and bite mankind because Raven wasn't allowed to marry a woman.

Now Raven had created the whole world. That is why he is never hunted because he made everything.

Beaver Story

It is tradition in many cultures for a boy's uncle to train him in the ways of a subsistence lifestyle. This is especially true of Alaskan cultural tradition. My uncle, Herbert Smelcer, still teaches me how to hunt caribou, of their habits, and where to find them. He also shows me where to fish in the Interior.

A very long time ago, it was time for a boy's uncle to teach him how to hunt and fish. For years the uncle tried to teach him, but the young boy was too lazy and liked to sleep all of the time. The uncle was tired of training the boy and wanted to get rid of him.

One day they went beaver hunting. They walked to a lake and chopped a hole through the top of a large beaver house. The beavers heard the chopping and swam away. The uncle told the boy to climb inside the house and wait inside because the beavers would return sometime.

"When they come back," the uncle told him, "you use your knife to kill them. When you are finished, I will come let you out."

The man replaced the top of the house and left for a while. When he returned to see if the boy had killed the beaver, he found him asleep.

The uncle was angry because the boy never learned anything and because he was so lazy. He quietly decided to re-cover the beaver house's roof again and leave the boy to die.

"Do not fall asleep this time," said the uncle. "I will come again in a few hours to get you."

But he did not come back. Instead, he headed back to the village, leaving the lazy boy to die.

The boy sat in the dark room for a long time and became very cold and hungry. He finally realized what had happened but he could not escape.

Just then, two beavers came up through the hole and saw the boy huddled on the floor.

"Look," they said. "There's a boy here. He must be lost and hungry."

So they cooked some food and spoke with him while he ate. The boy told him about his life in the village.

"You were left here because you have been so lazy and because you sleep all of the time," said one of the beavers.

When he was finished eating, the beavers made a hole in the roof so that the boy could escape.

126

"You will be a great hunter and a hard worker from now on," said the other beaver.

The boy thanked the two beavers and promised that he would never hunt or kill beavers for the rest of his life. Then he climbed out and ran home.

When he reached his village, the mean uncle was surprised—and scared. He could not imagine how the boy had escaped.

From that time on, though, the boy was a hard worker and a mighty hunter and all of the men respected him. But he never killed a single beaver in all of his life and no one ever knew why this was.

Old Man And Old Woman Rock

The following is a uniquely Han narrative which is somewhat similar to the Ahtna tale, "The Stone Woman". Too, it is a creation legend which recounts the origin of the Han Indian world. This particular narrative was first documented by F. Schmitter around 1909 or 1910.

Somewhere on the Yukon River between the village of Eagle and Fortymile there are two large, vertical rocks facing one another on either side of the mighty, silty river. Geologists say that long ago the rocks were connected but that some geological process split it and created the two features as we see them presently.

The stone near the north bank is called "Old Man" while that near the south bank is named "Old Woman" by the Han Indians. It is believed that these two were the very first Indians in the region a very long time ago.

It is said that they were married and that one day, while wading across the river, the couple split for one reason or another and went to different sides of the river. The husband went north while the wife went south.

In those days there were all kinds of animals; some were very unlike anything alive today, and they could speak just like men. The old man killed all of the mean ones and left only a few of the good ones which men would need to hunt in the future. Since he had killed almost all of the animals in the area, they forgot how to speak because they had no one else to talk to and that is why they do not talk today.

Before the old man and woman had gone to different sides of the Yukon, they had many children and they lived on both sides of the river hunting and fishing. That is why Indians live on both sides of the river.

When they died, the old man and the old woman turned into giant rocks which can still be seen today standing along the river.

He Who Flew To The Moon

Invariably, when humans looked up and saw the brilliant moon lighting the night sky, it seemed only natural that tales would eventually be told about it. Such accounts exist in folklore from around the world, including Eskimo. The following narrative appears in both Upper Tanana and Kutchin (Gwich'in) ethnography.

Once, a young Indian woman heard a baby crying in the woods and went to look for it, but she could not find it. Then another young woman heard the crying and she too went to find it, but she finally gave up as well. When the baby cried again, an old woman who had no children of her own went and found the baby in the middle of a hollow tree. She took him home with her and decided to raise him herself.

The old Indian woman was a good mother and the boy grew into a young man. Although he was a good son to the elderly woman, the boy was always playing tricks. In this sense he was a lot like Raven.

Now that the boy was a young man, and because she was getting too old, the woman decided to move to a nearby village where her brothers and cousins could help raise and instruct him.

After they had lived in her family's village only a short time, a man came running into camp saying that he had seen fifty caribou on a large, frozen lake nearby.

Everyone was excited and the young man who was adopted by the old woman said, "I will go and kill all of the caribou myself."

The villagers laughed because he had never hunted before. But early the next morning the young man started out towards where the animals were wearing an old, torn parka and worn out snowshoes. Nobody believed that he would even come close to the caribou, let alone kill a single one!

When the young man came upon the restless caribou, they saw him and always stayed just ahead of him so that he could not use his bow and arrows. An idea came to him, though. He took off his coat and old snowshoes and set them up over a small tree so that they looked like a man, then he started off towards the herd. Somehow, he was wearing a brand new parka and pair of snowshoes.

With his new clothes on, he caught up with and killed all fifty caribou! He walked back to the village and told them what he had done, but nobody believed him.

"I have killed them all!" he said.

Although they did not believe him, the men went to see for themselves. Soon, they came upon the lake and saw all of the dead caribou. They could not believe their eyes! Surely, they thought, the young man could not have killed all of these by himself. There was enough meat to last the entire village all winter.

While all of the men began gutting and cutting the caribou so that they could pack it out, the young man built a fire and after placing some caribou fat on his new snowshoes, he burned it in the flames. Then he ran around laughing aloud and singing. The other men thought he was silly and paid little attention to him.

Before they had finished with the caribou, the young man asked them to save some of the fat from each animal for him. But when they reached home no one gave him a single piece of fat. All he had was one very small piece which he found on the ground.

He was angry and hurt. He had killed all of the animals, yet no one gave him any of the fat. His old mother tried to comfort him, but she was unable to help.

Late that night, the young man jumped to his feet and held the small piece of fat over his head and began to fly off the ground! The old woman tried to grab his leg to pull him down, but she was not strong enough and so he kept flying upwards. He was flying to the moon! But before he flew there, he first killed all of the men in the village. From then on, he lived on the moon.

How Porcupine Got His Quills

Similar versions of this origin-myth occur throughout much of the Alaska interior Indian's oral histories. As the title suggests, this particular tale recounts how porcupines got their sharp quills.

When Porcupine was first created by Raven he had soft hair, not the sharp, protective quills like he now has.

Because he had no means to protect himself, Porcupine was always teased by the other animals, especially Bear and Wolf who bothered him the most. They would take his food away and leave him hungry, or they would harass him just for the fun of it.

This happened for many years and Porcupine learned a few ways to defend himself. One of his best tricks was to climb a tree so that his enemies could not reach him. But sometimes there was not a suitable tree nearby and so Bear or Wolf would take his food again. He was too slow to outrun most other animals, so he was really having a rough time of it.

One summer day, though, Bear and Wolf was teasing him and they shoved Porcupine into a mudhole. When poor Porcupine got out of the hole his soft hair was thick with muck. Bear and Wolf laughed at him and then they ran away with all of his food.

There was no river or lake nearby and so Porcupine could not wash the mud off. After a while, the hot summer sun dried the mud, making his hair all pointed and brittle.

Later that day, Bear saw Porcupine walking along a trail. When he came over to push him down as he had always done, he was quite surprised when his paws touched Porcupine's hair. Bear yelled in pain and ran away. Bear and Wolf never bothered him again. Since then, all porcupines have had sharp quills so that bigger animals cannot hurt them or take their food away from them as they used to.

When Raven Was Killed

My grandmother, Mary Wood, told me this story while I was video-taping her so that future generations and students could see that <u>how</u> a story is told is almost as important as the narrative itself. In my years of research, including the review of 148 texts, I have never before seen this particular tale. However, this does not imply that it does not exist in other Athabaskan traditions, only that I have not found it.

Raven had played so many tricks on mankind for so long that one day a great chief decided to kill him. The chief invited Raven to visit him and when the black bird wasn't watching, he quickly threw him into a large skin bag which he tied tightly shut so that the troublesome bird would not escape.

Then, with the large bag over his shoulder, the man began to climb a very high and steep mountain which was close by the village. It was very dark inside of the skin bag so Raven could not see anything. He asked the man what he was doing, but the chief ignored him.

As the chief climbed higher and higher, Raven spoke out again. "Where are you taking me?" he asked.

The chief just kept on climbing.

"I can tell that you are climbing a mountain," insisted Raven. "Why are you carrying me there? What are you going to do to me?"

The man ignored him still and continued to climb.

Raven warned the chief that he would be sorry if he killed him, saying that bad things would befall his people.

When the chief was on top of the mountain he threw the bag with Raven over the side. As it fell, it struck the side of the steep cliff and ripped open. Raven was torn to pieces by the jagged rocks as he crashed to the ground far below. The chief had killed Raven!

When the chief returned to his village, he showed the people the pieces of Raven so that they knew what he had done. All of the men called him a great chief for killing the mischievous trickster. For several days the villagers were happy and they celebrated.

Finally, though, some people started to notice that all of the water was gone. They went to the river, but it was dry. They went to a lake, but it was empty. There was no water to be found! Then the people began to get thirsty. They knew that they could not live long without water.

132

The people asked why the water had vanished and a shaman told them that it was gone because the chief had killed Raven. Now the villagers were not happy that Raven was dead and they wanted him back before everyone died.

The shaman told the chief that he had to put Raven back together. The chief took all of the pieces of the dead bird and put them together again. When he was finished Raven came back to life! He jumped up and started to fly away, but he first asked the chief why he had brought him back to life.

"All of the water has gone," the chief replied, "and only you can return it."

Raven flew up higher and then spoke to the man, "Look around you, there is water everywhere."

The chief turned and saw that the lake was full and that the river ran deep and fast again. As Raven disappeared in the distance, the chief promised never to try to kill Raven again.

Because of his powers and role in their heritage, natives do not kill ravens.

Bibliography

For further readings and information about Alaska Native mythologies and oral narratives, it is suggested that you read the following:

Tlingit

Ackerman, Maria. *Tlingit Stories.* Anchorage: Alaska Pacific University, 1975.

Alaska Quarterly Review. Vol. 4, No. 3 & 4. Ed. Tom F. Sexton, Ronald Spatz, James J. Liszka. Anchorage: University of Alaska Anchorage, 1986

Allen, Henry T. *Report of an Expedition to the Copper, Tanana, and Koyukon Rivers, in the Territory of Alaska, in the Year 1885.* Washington: GPO, 1887.

Beck, L. Mary. *Heroes & Heroines In Tlingit-Haida Legend.* Seattle: Alaska Northwest Books, 1989.

-----. *Shamans and Kushtakas.* Seattle: Alaska Northwest Books, 1991.

Bernet, John W., Ed. *An Anthology Of Aleut, Eskimo, And Indian Literature Of Alaska.* Fairbanks: UAF English Dept., 1974.

Carter, M. *Legends, Tales & Totems.* Palmer: Aladdin Press, 1975.

Dauenhauer, Nora and Richard. *Haa Shuka', Our Ancestors.* Juneau: University of Washington Press, 1987.

-----. *Haa Tuwunaaqu Yis: For Healing Our Spirit.* Seattle: Washington UP, 1990.

Dolch, Edward W. and Marguerite. *Stories From Alaska: Folklore of the World.* Illinois: Garrard Press, 1961.

Dundes, Alan. *Folklore Theses and Dissertations in the United States.* Austin: Texas UP, 1976.

Emmons, George T. *Memoirs of the American Museum of Natural History.* Vol. III, 1900-1907.

Feldmann, Susan. Ed. *The Story-Telling Stone.* New York: Dell, 1965. Reprinted 1991.

Hallock, Charles. *Our New Alaska.* New York: Forest And Stream Publishing Co., 1886.

Harris, Christie. *Once More Upon A Totem.* New York: Atheneum, 1973.

Harris, Lorle K. *Tlingit Tales.* California: Naturegraph, 1985.

Jonaitis, Aldona. *Art of the Northern Tlingit.* Seattle: University of Washington Press, 1986.

Jones, Livingston F. *A Study of the Thlingets of Alaska.* New York: Fleming H. Revell, 1914.

Kamenskii, Anatolii. *Tlingit Indians Of Alaska.* Trans. Sergei Kan. Fairbanks: University of Alaska Press, 1985.

Kapier, Dan and Nan Kapier. *Tlingit: Their Art, Culture & Legends.* Seattle: Hancock House, 1978.

Krause, Aurel. *The Tlingit Indians.* Trans. Erna Gunther. Seattle: Washington UP, 1970.

Krenov, Julia. "Legends from Alaska." *Journal de la Societe des Americanistes,* n.s. 40 (1951): 173-95.

Leer, J., Ed. *Tongass Texts.* Fairbanks: University of Alaska-Fairbanks Alaska Native Language Center, 1978.

Lynch, Kathleen. *Southeastern Stories.* Anchorage: Adult Literacy Laboratory, 1978.

Martin, Fran. *Nine Tales Of Raven.* New York: Harper & Row, 1951.

Mayol, Lurline B. *The Talking Totem Pole.* Portland: Binfords & Mort, 1943.

McClellan, Catherine. *The Girl Who Married The Bear: A Masterpiece of Indian Oral Tradition.* Ottawa: Canadian National Museum Publication, 1970.

McCorckle, Ruth. *The Alaska Ten Footed Bear And Other Legends.* Seattle: Robert D. Seal, 1958.

Norman, Howard. *Northern Tales: Traditional Stories of Eskimo and Indian Peoples.* New York: Pantheon Books, 1990.

Paul, Frances L. *Kahtahah.* Anchorage: Alaska Northwest, 1976.

Peck, Cyrus and Nadja Peck. *The Rocks Of Our Land Speak.* Juneau: Juneau-Douglas School District, 1977.

Peck, Cyrus E., Sr. *The Tides People.* Juneau: Indian Sutdies Program. Juneau School District, 1975.

Postell, Alice and A.P. Johnson. *Tlingit Legends*. Sitka: Sheldon Jackson Museum, 1986.

Smelcer, John. Ed. *The Raven and the Totem: An Anthology of Alaska Native Myths and Tales*. Anchorage: Salmon Run Publishers, 1992.

Swanton, John R. *Tlingit Myths and Texts*. Washington: U. S. Bureau of American Ethnology, 1909.

Trask, Willard R. *The Unwritten Song,* Vol. II . New York: Macmillian, 1967.

Velten, H. "Three Tlingit Stories." *International Journal of American Linquistics.* 10 (1944): 168-180.

Zuboff, Robert. *Kudatan Kahidee (The Salmon Box)*. Trans. Henry Davis. Sitka: Tlingit Readers, Inc., 1973.

-----. *Taax'aa (Mosquito)*. Ed. and Trans. Dick Dauenhauer. Fairbanks: A.N.L.C., 1973.

Eskimo

Ager, Lynn P. "Storytelling: an Alaskan Eskimo Girl's Game." *Journal of the Folklore Institute* 11, no. 3 (1974) : 189-98.

Alaska Quarterly Review. Vol. 4, No. 3 & 4. Ed. Tom F. Sexton, Ronald Spatz, James J. Liszka. Anchorage: University of Alaska Anchorage, 1986.

Balikci, Asen. *The Netsilik Eskimo*. Garden City: Natural History Press, 1970.

Bergsland, Knut. Ed. *Nunamiut Stories*. Barrow: North Slope Borough Commission on Inupiat History, 1987.

Bernet, John W., Ed. *An Anthology Of Aleut, Eskimo, And Indian Literature Of Alaska*. UAF: English Dept., 1974.

Birket-Smith, Kaj. "The Chugach Eskimo." Copenhagen: National-museets Publikationsfond, 1953.

Boas, Franz. "The Central Eskimo." *6th Annual Report of the Bureau of American Ethnology for the Years 1884-1885.* Washington, 1888. Reprint. Lincoln: Nebraska UP, 1964.

-----. *Mythology and Folktales of N. American Indians*. American Ethnological Society. Leiden: E. J. Brill, 1914.

-----. *Mythology and Folktales of N. American Indians.* American Ethnological Society. Leiden: E. J. Brill, 1914.

Bogoras, Waldemar. *Materials for the Study of the Chukchee Language and Folklore.* St. Petersburg: Imperial Academy of Science, 1900.

-----. *The Eskimo of Siberia.* Trans. Waldemar Bogoras. New York: AMS Press, 1913. Reprinted 1975.

Brown, Ticasuk Emily Ivanoff. *Tales of Ticasuk.* Fairbanks: University of Alaska Press, 1987.

-----. *The Longest Story Ever Told.* Anchorage: Alaska Pacific UP, 1981.

Carius, Helen S. *Sevukakmet.* Anchorage: Alaska Pacific UP, 1979.

Chugach Legends: Stories and Photographs of the Chugach Region. John F. C. Johnson, Compiler. Anchorage: Chugach Alaska Corporation, 1984.

Collins, Henry B. "Descriptions of the Polar Eskimo." *Handbook of North American Indians.* Vol. 5. Washington: Smithsonian (1985): 8.

DeArmond, Dale. *Berry Woman's Children.* New York: Greenwillow Books, 1985.

----. *The Boy Who Found The Light.* Boston: Little, Brown & Company, 1990.

-----. *The First Man: An Eskimo Folktale From Point Hope.* Sitka: Old Harbor Press, 1990.

Kawagley, Dolores. *Yupik Stories.* Anchorage: Alaska Methodist UP, 1975.

Keithahn, Edward L. *Alaskan Igloo Tales.* Seattle: Robert D. Seal, 1958.

Krauss, Michael E. *Native Peoples and Languages of Alaska.* Map. Fairbanks: Alaska Native Language Center, 1982.

Krenov, Julia. "Legends from Alaska." *Journal de la Societe des Americanistes,* n.s., 40 (1951):173-95.

Lantis, Margaret. "The Mythology of Kodiak Island, Alaska." *Journal of American Folklore* 51, no. 200 (1938):123-72.

Legends and Stories: Unipchaallu Uqaaqtuallu. Trans. Ruth R. Sampson. Anchorage: NBMDC, 1976.

Legends and Stories: Unipchaallu Uqaaqtuallu II. Trans. Ruth R. Sampson. Anchorage: NBMDC, 1978.

Long, Orma F. *Eskimo Legends.* Hicksville: Exposition Press, 1978.

Lucier, Charles B. "Noatagmiut Eskimo Myths." *Anthropological Papers of the University of Alaska* 6, no. 2 (1958): 89-117.

Lynch, Kathleen. *Northern Eskimo Stories.* Anchorage: Adult Literacy Laboratory, Anchorage Community College, 1978.

Maher, Ramona. *The Blind Boy and the Loon and Other Myths.* New York: John Day, 1969.

Mayokok, Robert. *Eskimo Stories.* Anchorage: Instant Printing.

Millman, Lawrence. *A Kayak Full Of Ghost: Eskimo Tales.* Santa Barbara: Capra Press, 1987.

McCorckle, Ruth. *The Alaska Ten Footed Bear And Other Legends.* Seattle: Robert D. Seal, 1958.

Nanogak, Agnes. *More Tales from the Igloo.* Edmonton: Hurtig, 1986.

Nelson, Edward W. "The Eskimo About Bering Strait." *18th Annual Report of the Bureau of American Ethnology.* GPO, 1899.

Norman, Howard. *Northern Tales: Traditional Stories of Eskimo and Indian Peoples.* New York: Pantheon Books, 1990.

Oman, Lela Kiana. *Eskimo Legends.* Anchorage: Alaska Methodist UP, 1975.

Oquilluk, William A. *People Of Kauwerak: Legends Of The Northern Eskimo.* Anchorage: Alaska Methodist UP, 1973.

Rasmussen, Knud. *The Eagle's Gift: Alaska Eskimo Tales.* Trans. Isobel Hutchinson. New York: Doubleday & Doran, 1932.

-----. *Eskimo Folk Tales.* Ed. and Trans. W. Worster. Copenhagen: Gyldendal, 1921.

Rink, Hinrich J. *Tales And Traditions Of The Eskimo.* Ed. Robert Brown. London: William Blackwood & Sons, 1875.

Silook, Roger S. *Seevookuk: Stories the Old People Told on St. Lawrence Island.* Anchorage: Alaska Publishing Company, 1976.

Smelcer, John E. *The Caribou and the Stone Man.* Anchorage: Grayling Press, 1991.

-----. *The Raven and the Totem: An Anthology of Alaska Native Myths and Tales.* Anchorage: Salmon Run Publishers, 1992.

Spencer, Robert F. *The North Alaskan Eskimo: A Study in Ecology and Society.* *Bureau of American Ethnology Bulletin* no. 171. Washington, 1959. Reprinted in 1969.

Stefansson, Viljalmur. "Report of Stefansson-Anderson Arctic Expedition." *Anthropological Papers of the American Museum of Natural History.* Vol. XIV. New York, 1919.

Sverdrup, Harald U. *Among The Tundra People.* Trans. Molly Sverdrup. Regents of University of California, 1978.

Tennant, Edward A. and Joseph N. Bitar, Ed. *Yupik Lore: Oral Traditions of an Eskimo People.* Bethel: LKSD, 1981.

Trask, Willard R. *The Unwritten Song.* New York: Macmillan, 1967.

Whittaker, C. E. *Arctic Eskimo: A Record of Fifty Years' Experience & Observation Among The Eskimo.* London: Seeley, Service & Co., 1937. Reprinted 1976.

Wilder, Edna. *Once Upon An Eskimo Time.* Edmonds: Alaska Northwest Publishing Company, 1987.

Woodbury, Anthony C. *CEV'ARMIUT QANEMCIIT QULIRAIT-LLU: Eskimo Narratives and Tales from Chevak, Alaska.* Fairbanks: University of Alaska Press, 1984.

-----. *Life in the Quasgiq. In Inua: Spirit World of the Bering Sea Eskimo.* Washington, D. C.: Smithsonian, 1982.

Athabaskan

Alaska Quarterly Review. Vol. 4, No. 3 & 4. Ed. Tom F. Sexton, Ronald Spatz, James J. Liszka. Anchorage: University of Alaska Anchorage, 1986.

Allen, Henry T. *Report of an Expedition to the Copper, Tanana, and Koyukon Rivers, in the Territory of Alaska, in the Year 1885.* Washington: GPO, 1887.

Atna' Yanida'a (Ahtna Stories). Trans. Millie Buck. Anchorage: National Bilingual Materials Development Center, 1979.

Attla, Catherine. *As My Grandfather Told It: Traditional Stories from the Koyukuk.* Alaska: Yukon-Koyukuk School District and the Alaska Native Language Center (UAF), 1983.

-----. *Stories We Live By: Traditional Koyukon Athabaskan Stories.* Fairbanks: Alaska Native Language Center (UAF) and the Yukon-Koyukuk School District, 1989.

Bernet, John W., Ed. *An Anthology of Aleut, Eskimo, And Indian Literature Of Alaska.* Fairbanks: UAF English Dept., 1974.

Boas, Franz, Ed. *Mythology and Folk-tales of N. American Indians.* American Ethnological Society. Leiden: E. J. Brill, 1914.

Brean, Alice. *Athabascan Stories.* Anchorage: Alaska Methodist UP, 1975.

Chapman, John W. *Athabaskan Stories From Anvik.* Ed. and Trans. James Kari. Fairbanks: ANLC, 1981.

-----. "Athabascan Traditions from the Lower Yukon." *Journal of American Folklore* 15, no. 62 (1903): 180-85.

-----. *Ten'a Texts and Tales from Anvik, Alaska.* American Ethnological Society no. 6. Leyden: E. J. Brill, 1914.

Cruickshank, Julie. *Athabaskan Women: Lives and Legends.* Ottawa: Canadian National Museum of Man, Mercury Series, Ethnology Service Paper no. 57, 1979.

De Laguna, Frederica, and Marie-Francoise Guedon. "Ahtna Fieldnotes." Manuscripts in author's possession. Microfilm copy at American Philosophical Society, Philadelphia, 1968.

Deacon, Belle. *Their Stories of Long Ago.* Ed. James Kari. Fairbanks: ANLC and the Iditarod Area School District, 1987.

DOTSON' SA TAALEEBAAY LAATLGHAAN (How Raven Killed The Whale). Trans. Eliza Jones. Fairbanks: ANLC.

Dundes, Alan. *Folklore Theses and Dissertations in the United States.* Austin: Texas UP, 1976.

Fredson, John and Edward Sapir. *Kutchin texts with translations, 1923.* Ethnology Division Archives, National Museum Of Man, Ottawa, Canada.

Greene, Diana S. *Raven Tales & Medicine Men Folktales From Eagle Village.* 1988. No other data available.

Guedon, Marie-Francoise. *People of Tetlin, Why Are You Singing?* Canadian National Museum of Man, Mercury Series, Ethnology Service Paper no. 9. Ottawa, 1974.

Herbert, Belle. *Shandaa: In My Lifetime.* Ed. Bill Pfisterer. Fairbanks: ANLC, 1982.

Jette, Jules. "On Ten'a Folk-Lore." *Journal of the Royal Anthropological Institute of Great Britain and Ireland,* n.s., 38 (1908):298-367; 39 (1909):460-505.

Kalifornsky, Peter. *K'TL'EGH'I SUKDUA (Remaining Stories).* Fairbanks: ANLC, 1984.

Kari, James. Ed. *A Dena'ina Legacy: The Collected Writtngs Of Peter Kalifornsky.* Fairbanks: ANLC, 1991.

-----. *Tatl'ahwt' aenn Nenn': The Headwaters People's Country.* Fairbanks: ANLC, 1986.

-----. *Ts' eba Tthadala': The First Christmas Tree Story.* Fairbanks: ANLC, 1991.

Keim, Charles J., Ed. "Kutchin Legends From Old Crow." *Anthropological Papers of the University of Alaska* 11 (1964): 9.

Krauss, Michael E., Ed. *Native Peoples and Languages of Alaska.* Map. Fairbanks: ANLC, 1974. Reprinted 1982.

Krenov, Julia. "Legends from Alaska." *Journal de la Societe des Americanistes,* n.s., 40 (1951): 173-95.

Lohr, Amy L., Ed. *Athabaskan Story-Teaching: Gaither D. Paul Stories.* Alaska Historical Commission Studies in History, No. 183., 1985.

Mackenzie, Clara C. *Zhoh Gwatsan: Wolf Smeller.* Anchorage: Alaska Pacific UP, 1985.

Mishler, Craig. Ed. *Kutchin Tales.* Trans. Moses P. Gabriel. Anchorage: Adult Literacy Library, 1973.

Nelson, Richard K. *Make Prayers to the Raven: A Koyukon View of the Northern Forest.* Chicago: Chicago Press, 1989.

Norman, Howard. *Northern Tales: Traditional Stories of Eskimo and Indian Peoples.* New York: Pantheon, 1990.

Osgood, Cornelius. *Contributions to the Ethnography of the Kutchin.* New Haven: Yale University Publication in Anthropology, No. 14 (1936), 1970.

-----. *The Ethnography of the Tanaina.* New Haven: Yale University Publication in Anthropology, 1937.

Paul, Gaither. *Stories for my Grandchildren*. Ed. Ron Scollon. Fairbanks: ANLC, 1980.

Peter, Katherine and Mary L. Pope. Ed. *Dinjie Zhuu Gwandak: Gwich'in Stories*. Anchorage: Alaska State Operated Schools, 1974. Reprint.

Peters, Henry. *NAY' NADELIGHA I'GHAAN DGHSAT 'AEN'DEN (The War At Nay'nadeli)*. Trans. and Ed. James Kari. Fairbanks: ANLC, 1977.

Q'udi Heyi Nilch'diluyi Sukdu'a (This Year's Collected Stories). Trans. and Ed. James Kari. Anchorage: N.B.M.D.C., 1980.

Ridley, Ruth. *EAGLE HAN HUCH'INN HODOK (Stories in Eagle Han Huch'inn)*. Fairbanks: ANLC, 1983.

Schmitter, Ferdinand. *Upper Yukon Native Customs and Folk-Lore*. Washington: Smithsonian Collections, vol. 56, no. 4, 1906. Reprinted 1985.

Smelcer, John. *The Caribou and the Stone Man*. Anchorage: Grayling Publishers, 1991.

-----. *The Raven and the Totem: An Anthology of Alaska Native Myths and Tales*. Anchorage: Salmon Run Publishers, 1992.

Tildzidza Hwzoya' (Mouse Story). Told by Alta Jerue. Trans. Betty Petruska. McGrath: Iditarod Area School District, 1990.

Tenenbaum, Joan M. *Denan'ina Sukdu'a: Traditional Stories of the Tanaina Athabaskans*. Ed. Mary J. McGary. Fairbanks: ANLC, 1984.

Vaudrin, Bill. *Tanaina Tales from Alaska*. Norman: Oklahoma UP, 1969.

Wassillie, Albert, Jr. *Nuvendaltun Ht'ana Sukdu'a (Nondalton People's Stories)*. Ed. James Kari. Anchorage: N.B.M.D.C., 1980.

ABOUT THE ARTISTS

John E. Smelcer, who was recently a Guest Native American Scholar at the Gorky Institute of World Literature in Moscow, Russia, at Brooklyn College, New York, and at the University of Wisconsin-Eau Claire, teaches English at Embry-Riddle Aeronautical University. His books of poetry include *The Caribou and the Stone Man, Koht'aene Kenaege', Kesugi Ridge,* and *Changing Seasons.* He edited *Durable Breath: Contemporary Native American Poetry,* an anthology featuring forty-three major Native American poets. He is the author of three books on Alaska Native mythology. His autobiographical essay appears in *Everything Matters: Autobiographical Essays By Native American Writers.* One of his poems appears in *The Wall That Stands,* an international volume of Native American poetry. His work has been nominated for the Pulitzer Prize, the William Carlos Williams Award, and a Pushcart Prize. His poetry has most recently appeared in *The American Voice, The Atlantic Monthly, The Amicus Journal, Artful Dodge, The Beloit Poetry Journal, The Christian Science Monitor, Faultline, International Poetry Review, The Kenyon Review, The Literary Review, Poet, Rosebud,* and ZYZZYVA.

Larry Vienneau teaches art at the University of Alaska in Fairbanks. His artwork has won national recognition and recently appeared in exhibit in Hong Kong. In 1992 he received the *Best of Painting Award* at the All Alaska Juried Art Show. His wife Suhtling and he are mad fishermen, doing anything in the name of fishing. Suht is a film-editor and producer.

Susie Qimmiqsak Bevins, of Aleut heritage, is a respected artist living in Anchorage with her husband Kris Ericson. Many public buildings showcase her artwork and sculptures.

Other Books By the Author

In The Shadows of Mountains: Ahtna
Indian Stories From the Copper River
        With Pulitzer Prize author, Gary Snyder

A Cycle Of Myths: Native Legends
From Southeast Alaska

Tracks
        With Pulitzer Prize author, Carl Sagan

Durable Breath: Contemporary Native
American Poetry
        With Don Birchfield

Changing Seasons: New & Selected Poems